Beyond Sorry

How to Own Up, Make Good, and Move Forward After a Crisis

Ray Hennessey

Fulton Books
Meadville, PA

Published by Fulton Books 2024

ISBN 979-8-88982-793-1 (paperback)
ISBN 979-8-88982-794-8 (digital)

Printed in the United States of America

Contents

Introduction
Bad People vs. Bad Actions..v
Going beyond Sorry ix
Do the Work xi

Chapter 1: Why Apologize?
The Era of the Apology 1
Why Do Apologies Help? 8
What Does Sorry Even Mean? 13

Chapter 2: Owning It
Taking Ownership...18
Avoiding Denial 22
Examining Our Conscience...28

Chapter 3: Finding the Right Words
Being Genuine 32
Framework over Formula 36
Speaking with Empathy..43

Chapter 4: Delivering the Message
Know Your Audience...49
The First Seven Seconds 53
The Public Apology...60

Chapter 5: The Ideal of Forgiveness
Why It's So Hard...65
Why People Don't Forgive...68
Forgiving Yourself..72

Chapter 6: Moving Forward

Believing You're Capable..77

Moving from Shame to Accountability..............................81

Living Worthy of Redemption...87

Chapter 7: When Not to Apologize

Are You Really Sorry? 96

Sorry, Not Sorry...104

The Long Arm of the Law..107

Your Comeback...109

Introduction

Bad People vs. Bad Actions

The client I was about to meet never thought he'd make front-page news. A young, up-and-coming financial professional, he was in that gloaming where the behaviors of college and your early twenties should have been giving way to the stability and routine of adulthood. But old habits were dying hard, and the impulse to let loose spilled over into a raging party with so much sexual excess and property damage that it easily became fodder for the New York tabloids. The client was quickly fired by the conservative financial firm where he worked, mostly because of traditional and social media pressure to treat him as a pariah. With the double whammy of a loss of significant income and deep embarrassment, he needed help. So through a referral, he found his way to my firm at the time, which had an unmatched reputation for helping companies and individuals navigate the media storms of their own mistakes to come out the other side with minimal damage and very often stronger than they were before.

While my firm was well-known, this line of work was all new to me. I'd spent twenty-five years in media as a reporter, editor, and television presenter. My job had been to find newsworthy scandals and play them up. "If it bleeds, it leads," as the old saying went. Journalism at its heart is about finding conflict and getting as many people as possible to watch, listen, and read about it. Now I'd crossed over to the other side and was about to stand face-to-face with exactly the kind of media target I would have savaged in my past life.

There was something intensely personal about this work—and this client—for me. Like everyone else, I'd made huge mistakes in my life. I lost a job because of immaturity. I was on my third marriage. I lost friends and alienated some family along the way. I lied with astonishing frequency and ease. Like the song, I went looking for love in all the wrong places. In all those low points in my life, I felt that I could never recover. I felt at times like my life and career were both over. I felt shame. I felt sorrow, and I felt sorry. I hated myself for the things I'd done and said to people I loved and respected. Through it all, though, I still engaged in the punishment that media metes out on people who stray from what society deems to be the "right" path. I was a hypocrite for years.

Then I was faced with this client, and I immediately was reminded of a concept that had been missing from my thinking for far too long: redemption. Growing up Irish Catholic, one would think that redemption isn't something I would have needed to be reminded of. It's the basis of my faith, after all. In fact, it's the basis of most religions. But being Catholic most of my life, and then marrying into a Jewish family and raising Jewish children, I was more surrounded by the concept of guilt and sin. We're humans, and humans do wrong. It's life. In one of his first interviews, Pope Francis was asked what people should know about him. "I am a sinner," he said. "I am sure of this."

It was sin I was raised to be aware of. And it was everywhere. As I matured, I realized how commonplace bad behavior was. I often thought about Warren Zevon's 1991 song "Mr. Bad Example," which crystalized how all humans behave:

> I'm very well acquainted with the seven deadly sins.
> I keep a busy schedule trying to fit them in.
> I'm proud to be a glutton and I don't have time for sloth.
> I'm greedy and I'm angry and I don't care who I cross.

Did all of this mean that people are just inherently bad? It was more than a philosophical question. My profession in media and then in crisis and public relations was surrounded by the implications of how humans perceive bad behavior in others. More and more, people were getting caught up in what was being called cancel culture, where someone's misdeeds not only were laid bare, but there was also intense pressure to punish by taking away someone job or platform. If you were a brand or executive who stepped out of line, not only would your company face the typical pressure to take action, but social media mobs would reach out to clients or advertisers and demand that they too join in the outrage. It wasn't just companies and executives, either. With social media, personal failings among people who weren't even in the public eye could be exposed. Reclaiming your reputation after a crisis, whether professional or personal, has become more important than ever before because your actions are seen and judged by more people than ever before. In some cases, friends and family are openly debating or attacking you on places like Facebook in front of hundreds of other people. Nothing is private anymore. Despite all that's written about finding separation between work and life, there really isn't any. If you get arrested for drunken driving on your own time, your employer, clients, and customers are more likely to see it online and more likely feel pressure to take action.

My biggest problem with the focus on people's wrongdoing was that it automatically assumed that the person doing wrong was somehow inherently bad. Instead of bad *actions*, we're judging bad *people*. When we decide someone is bad, it's harder to believe we can ever trust them again. I've just never believed that most people are inherently bad. Everyone does something wrong. Everyone. Everyone has something in their past that they hide or are ashamed of. But people themselves just aren't normally bad. They just make mistakes. And in my mind at least, the vast majority of people deserve additional chances to let the good shine through. People deserve a chance at redemption. Helping people to find that second chance seemed like a good job for me.

That brought me back to our client. Did he deserve another chance? His mistakes fell into the categories of drunken excess and bad judgment. No one was physically hurt. No one was robbed. He was here not asking how to get away with what he had done but how to recover from it. He was asking for a second chance. He was asking for people to not judge him so harshly. I had to decide, as someone paid to help him get his next chance, whether he was worthy of that chance. Our team had the necessary media push covered. We expertly planned a roadshow on television and in the tabloids to give a counternarrative, and I was confident that our approach was the right one. But the success of that campaign rested on whether anyone would believe the guy in front of me. If he wasn't genuine in explaining his side of the story, he would fail. Most importantly, I needed to believe him.

I decided on a tactic I'd used in the past to test people. We were in our Manhattan office's corner conference room on Fifth Avenue. I was standing with my back to him, staring out the window.

"Just sit down," I said. No hello. No handshake. I'm not sure I even moved.

"Okay," he said. I then let there be some seconds of silence.

"You are an awful person," I said to him, turning to him for the first time. "You represent all that's wrong with Wall Street and finance. You're why people complain about the 1 percent. You're why people talk about white privilege. You're why people think hedge funds are evil. You deserve to lose your job, and you deserve all the hate you're getting."

He was quiet for a few seconds. And then he looked at me and said, "You're right."

It was the answer I was hoping to get. I smiled.

"We can work with you," I said. "Nothing I just said was true. You're not bad. You just made a dumb decision and got caught up in something that got out of control. I needed to see that you wouldn't naturally go on the defensive when people ask tough questions on TV. I wanted to see whether you were actually sorry. Are you?"

"Oh, I'm sorry," he said. "I'm beyond sorry."

Going beyond Sorry

Being sorry about what you did actually is the first step to proving to the world that you deserve that chance. Being sorry should prove to you and to others that you're not a bad person or an awful colleague. You're just a regular, flawed human who engaged in bad behavior, behavior that embarrasses you most of all. That's the opening gambit, an apology that acknowledges what you've done wrong and starts you on the path to reclaiming trust and your reputation. But that path, as my client suggested, requires you to go beyond sorry.

I'm no psychologist, theologian, or therapist, but I've done years of research on what it means to go beyond simply apologizing to get to a place where you could truly move forward with your life, your career, and your family. Looking at music, literature, religion, art, politics, and theater, I found that we're surrounded by stories about bad moves, apologies, and redemption. That isn't surprising, given who we are. As human beings, we're naturally flawed. We'll always make mistakes. We will always make a bad move. We will lie, cheat, or steal. We have Darwinian instincts and psychological trauma that makes us unfaithful, prideful, and greedy. It's life.

Being able to move forward from all those bad actions is a condition of survival. We can't simply live unhappily ever after. We need additional chances in order to evolve. And that's what going beyond sorry is: an evolution. You can't change overnight. When you make a mistake, you need to really understand why, face up to those you've hurt, examine yourself, and change the characteristics in yourself that got you into hot water in the first place. Then the work doesn't stop. You have to live a life worthy of the changes you made in yourself, all in an effort to regain trust.

You can be successful in this. Anyone who has lost a job or a marriage knows the personal desolation that follows. We mourn our past and can't get our minds around what the future will look like. It's hard to believe we can ever come back. But we can.

In my office, I have a photo of Raymond Donovan, the former Reagan Administration Secretary of Labor, who was indicted on corruption charges for his work with a construction company accused of having mob ties. The media had a field day with Donovan. After all, it wasn't every day you could paint a Reagan cabinet member as a Mafia stooge.

I was fascinated by Donovan as a kid. He grew up in my own hometown of Bayonne, New Jersey, and was friendly with my grandparents. He was a local boy made good. It was personal when I saw what he was going through. And boy, did he suffer. Despite the allegations and the media pile-on, the charges against Donovan didn't hold up. In fact, Donovan's attorneys actually never put up a defense. They rested their case without calling a single witness, saying the prosecution failed to prove Donovan did anything wrong. The jury in the case agreed, and Donovan walked out a free man.

Shortly afterward, Donovan asked a question to the media that made him famous: "Which office do I go to get my reputation back?"

Donovan was innocent. Not everyone is. (You likely aren't, or else you wouldn't be reading this book.) Your reputation has been harmed because people don't screw up in silence in a digital age. Each day, there are headlines about executives losing their jobs because of workplace misconduct. What's more, social media magnifies people's misdeeds, creating a digital footprint that can alert people to incidents years in the past. That affects the ability to find new work and do business in the future.

We spend a lifetime building our reputation, but though we think reputations are made of brick and mortar, they're more like a house of sticks, vulnerable to a huffing, puffing breath of wind. We can be defamed easily, finding ourselves on the defensive in the most improbable moments. We can make one bad decision and be judged by it for the rest of our lives. We can (rightly) be called out for awful chronic behavior that was ignored in the past. Sometimes, we can actually do everything right, but one unfounded accusation can define us.

Reclaiming your reputation isn't a question of applying to an office. It's a question of changing hearts, minds, and opinions. When you've done wrong, you can rebuild your reputation by proving to people that your apology is more than words. That's what it means to go beyond sorry.

Do the Work

This isn't easy, and success isn't guaranteed. You've likely broken some bond of trust to get here. You cheated on a spouse. You've lied. You've engaged in inappropriate behavior. Your actions have naturally alienated you from communities that previously showed you love and support. You have to put faith in yourself to do the work. Be prepared to suffer even more loss along the way because chances are, to go beyond sorry, you have to let go of people and habits that will tempt you to slide back to your worst impulses. Author Brianna Wiest, in her book *The Mountain Is You: Transforming Self-Sabotage Into Self-Mastery*, crystallizes the loss and gain in front of you:

> Your new life is going to cost you your old one. It's going to cost you your comfort zone and your sense of direction. It's going to cost you relationships and friends. It's going to cost you being liked and understood. It doesn't matter. The people who are meant for you are going to meet you on the other side. You're going to build a new comfort zone around the things that actually move you forward. Instead of being liked, you're going to be loved. Instead of being understood, you're going to be seen. All you're going to lose is what was built for a person you no longer are.

If you're ready to trade these losses for gains, then it's time to go beyond sorry. There's no magic formula to earn back trust or forgiveness or rebuild your reputation, but there is a process to undergo to set you back on the right path. We live in a world where people attack, but they also reconcile. Go beyond sorry, and you will come out stronger than before.

Chapter 1

Why Apologize?

The Era of the Apology

Life means always having to say you're sorry.

That may be a bit of an overstatement and an unfair bastardization of Erich Segal's famous line about love, but it certainly seems that we have a bumper crop of apologies nowadays. From politicians to media figures to entertainers to just plain regular folks, we find ourselves regularly seeing people make apologies for things they've done or said. It's tempting to ask whether we live in an era of people just behaving badly more, making it more necessary to try to fix relationships with a parade of apologies.

We aren't behaving any worse or better than we have in history. We are human, and part of being human is screwing up. All day long. Early and often. People have behaved badly for as long as humans have walked the earth. Screwing up is so commonplace that we have, in business circles, damn near fetishized failure as if it's the only or best path to achieving success. You can't learn from mistakes if you don't make them after all. But our failures, personal and professional, are often avoidable. Very often, when we're accused of saying the wrong thing, we *know* we shouldn't say something before the words come out of our mouth. When we do something wrong, we do it with the knowledge that our actions are wrong. Sure, we might learn from the outcomes. We may be fired or reprimanded or face some

1

penalty, but we learn more from the consequences of our actions than from the actions themselves. We find ourselves sorry very often for being caught rather than having truly done wrong.

Again, that's human nature. History is full of examples of people engaging in behavior they knew was wrong and did it anyway. What's more, as humans, we've always loved the stories of people screwing up big-time. The Bible starts with Adam and Eve, both of whom were told the rules very clearly but gave into the temptation of the fruit. Many religious texts have the same undertones. Greek mythology rivals the darkest imaginations of any horror novelist. Zeus, king of the gods, was awful. He killed his first wife to marry Hera; he routinely raped humans who resisted his advances, engaged in fairly regular incest, and spent a lot of time alternately helping and harming his fellow gods and humans. Modern monotheistic traditions define God as perfection, but the gods of old were more representative of the worst of our behaviors.

Vengeance has been a common theme in history too. Again, Zeus, probably without giving a thought to irony, meted out some of the worst punishments in literature. Tantalus, Zeus's mortal son, stole ambrosia from the gods and served up his own dead son to them to eat and was thus punished to a life in the underworld where he had a fruit tree above him and a pool of water below him—and both moved out of reach every time he was trying to sate his eternal hunger and thirst. (We get the word *tantalize* from this.) When Prometheus gave fire to humankind, he was punished by being chained to a rock and having his liver pecked at by an eagle every night.

Shakespeare's tragedies are all about our fatal flaws. Othello's was jealousy, which led him to kill his wife. King Lear suffered from arrogance, ignorance, and excessive pride. Macbeth's was his ambition. Hamlet had so many flaws they're still debated in high school term papers today. Those flaws led to downfalls. Those flaws are also common in all of us. Characters in literature mimic our character in life. When we have a reputational, professional, or personal problem, it's generally because of our own flaws (hopefully not fatal). But because our tendency to make mistakes or do wrong to people is so much a part of human nature, we should first take solace in knowing that no matter what we've done, someone somewhere has done something worse. That doesn't excuse whatever we've done to get us in trouble, but it does remind us that you're in a club that has spanned millennia.

Also, in our very human nature, we have a tendency to not only make mistakes ourselves but to revel in the errors of others. That's why mythology and literature is full of crime and punishment in all cultures. We see the flaws of others as a reflection of ourselves, but we also enjoy seeing people get their comeuppance. And if we don't exactly enjoy the suffering of others, we at least mourn it because we understand that flaws are inevitable, and often, our first instinct is forgiveness. When Horatio leans over Hamlet and says, "Good night, sweet prince, and flights of angels sing thee to thy rest!" he does so in forgiveness and mourning for all of us.

Notice that amid all the literature around flaws, mistakes, and dark and dirty deeds, there appear to be very few apologies. There are very few great orations from leaders in history where they admit fault. In fact, there are more justifications than apologies. The few apologies in history come from religious texts, but even they are often delivered weakly, certainly not in the same league as the bad acts worthy of apology. So why now does it seem today that every time we turn around, someone is saying sorry for something?

It's that our own flaws (known as *harmatia* in Greek tragedies) are much more out in the open because our lives are more out in the open. With the prevalence of social media, we're living our lives less in the quietude of our own home and more among the cacophony of a digital world. What was private is now public. Our friends know our breakups—and too often the reasons for them—because of Facebook status updates. Our LinkedIn profiles show our job losses. News travels faster than we are often able to handle it, and bad news has always traveled faster than the good.

We are also more likely to make a reputation-damaging miscue in front of people in this environment. Words or actions that might have prompted a shake of the head in a private conversation become the stuff of anonymous scorn on social media.

The most infamous example was Justine Sacco, a public relations professional, who in 2013 was a thirty-year-old with Twitter on her smartphone and a trip to her family in South Africa from New York on her itinerary.

Among a number of tweets that showed sufficient snark for a person fresh from their twenties, Sacco wrote, "Going to Africa. Hope I don't get AIDS. Just kidding. I'm white!" She then, as people do on an eleven-hour flight, promptly fell asleep.

What she didn't know was that her tweet was heard 'round the world while she snored away. A reporter, Sam Biddle, from the *Valleywag* website saw it and highlighted it. What followed were tens of thousands of tweets and retweets calling Sacco racist. It was so much that Sacco's employer at the time, Internet conglomerate IAC, weighed in: "This is an outrageous, offensive comment. Employee in question currently unreachable on an intl flight." (She would later be fired for it.) Sacco had no idea any of this was happening as she flew to Cape Town. By the time she landed, Sacco had become the most hated and ridiculed woman on the Internet—and there was even a stranger waiting in the airport to snap a photo of her and post it, confirming she had indeed landed.

L'affaire Sacco was by technological design, not by chance. It's important to remember that for all the good that social media has done in making communications among humanity easier, it is also a business. And as author Douglas Rothkoff has put so eloquently, rather than being consumers of this technology, we are actually the product. Social media is a giant real-time reality show where we're both the players and the audience. Our lives provide the drama, and we are subject to the acceptance, revulsion, appreciation, disappointment, and anger of any actor on a stage. Sacco, while she slept on the flight, had become a star of this show. Hashtags were created to encourage her to be fired, others to ask whether her plane had landed. People parsed and argued over the meaning of her words like sages over a sacred text. It became a worldwide carnival atmosphere, tweets and retweets flying, all from people who had no idea who Justine Sacco even was. I recall sitting at a restaurant while I was editorial director of *Entrepreneur Magazine* at the time and a colleague asking if I weighed in on the Justine Sacco issue yet. Who? And why the hell would I want to weigh in on someone I had never even met?

In retrospect, the incident could look like a massive invasion of privacy and personal space. But it wasn't—at least from a legal standpoint. Like all of us who log into a social network, we give up many rights. With apologies to Pierre Teilhard de Chardin, SJ, we are collaborators in this social creation. For the opportunity to post our kids' soccer pictures or to opine in a tweet about an election, we sign away rights to our privacy that may otherwise exist. We join this actors' union as willing participants for better or for worse, 'til death, deactivation, or deplatforming do us part. Worse, we do it so casually, agreeing to small-font terms and conditions most of us never even read.

That's created a shift in how we view who is in the public eye. Politicians have always known that they're giving up some kind of expectations of privacy when they become a public figure. It's the same with business leaders who run public companies. When you have stakeholders to hold you accountable, your actions and words naturally come under more scrutiny. In fact, under libel law, being a public figure gives the media more leeway in how they can write about you and limits your ability to win a lawsuit if you think you have been unfairly attacked by the press. That's an open societal trade-off. People who rise to the point in their lives and their careers where they seek attention and strive to become public figures know what they're getting themselves into. I've counseled clients who are seeking broad media exposure that such attention always comes with a price. You are exposing yourself to public scrutiny, and the public can turn against you, ascribe bias, and motives to your words and really come after you, so you have to be ready. It's just part of the stage you're choosing to be on.

But regular folks dumb-thumbing on social often don't realize that they too are now public figures. On open platforms like Twitter, Instagram, or Snapchat, unless you are actively keeping your posts private, many people can see them. You don't know your audience. You may think you're only speaking to your friends, but you're not. In fact, you should know better. Some of us seek validation in counting how many followers or friends we have on these platforms as if those are data points for our self-worth, not realizing that nothing could be further from the truth. These followers don't know you, and you don't know them. Sacco, whose tweets were known to be biting and sarcastic, was happened upon by a stranger who was offended, and that stranger made the most of his shot.

Put aside that Sacco's subsequent explanation made her seem far more thoughtful about the comment. Rather than racist, she told *The New York Times Magazine*, it was a statement about white privilege. "To put it simply," she said, "I wasn't trying to raise awareness of AIDS or piss off the world or ruin my life. Living in America puts us in a bit of a bubble when it comes to what is going on in the third world. I was making fun of that bubble."

Yes, there is always context to our words and actions. Trouble is, context never RSVP'd to the social media party. When you say or write words or commit an act, the audience gets to make judgments for you. That's actually part of the reward for being the audience. Remember the Hamlet example? For centuries, we've been trying to determine what his problem really was. And our own personal interpretation makes the play personal to us. That may be lost to us in our first high school reading, but for those who come back to it later after heartache, drama, failings and experience, we see it and own the story in a different way. That's why we find so much beauty in art and literature and relationships. We see things in our own way, interpret art through our own personal lens, and allow it to speak to us in our own language. With social media as a drama, we view words and actions through our own lens. Your context for an inappropriate statement or post or the true meaning behind something you said during a speech or even the legitimate excuse you broke the law or dishonored a vow doesn't matter because that's not how drama works. When you bare yourself to the world, you are at the mercy of the crowd. And mercy is never first on the crowd's mind.

If the story ended there, it would indeed be tragedy. We would have to live with an ending in our lives and our reputations where the curtain falls on nothing but pain. Indeed, as we view how the media at large dramatizes our lives and our behaviors, we forget that there are true humans, not actors, with real feelings at stake here. In a book on public shaming, Sacco showed the depth of the pain the incident caused her, recalling that she "cried out my body weight in the first twenty-four hours."

But unlike Greek tragedy, life goes on, and the curtain doesn't go down. Life is more like a cheesy soap opera rather than a grand production. Characters who are killed off suddenly come back years later. Plotlines change frequently. Most importantly, heroes become villains and villains become heroes. Life doesn't end, so the show must go on. Despite all the rhetoric around "cancel culture," almost nobody's reputation is in the dumpster forever.

That's where apologies come in. Apologies are the first step toward, if not forgiveness, then reacceptance into the communities our actions shattered. They are so prevalent because they tend to work. At bottom, we focus on the worst part of the cycle after our misdeeds—the yelling, the opprobrium, the digital torches and pitchforks of the anonymous social media mob. Yet the fire of anger, hurt, and public shaming almost always dies down. An apology may not be accepted at first, but the fact that it's offered shows people that you're truly sorry, that you accept the consequences, are ready to learn, and are ready to change. An apology allows you not only to speak to your detractors but to also allow your defenders and supporters to more willingly readmit you into their circles. An apology allows people to create a frame of reference to keep you accountable for the future. An apology lets you get back on the path of getting your life back.

This is a country and world of second chances. I say that so much that folks around me often roll their eyes. But as much as our media-driven world loves to tear down people, it also loves to watch a comeback story. It loves to see growth. So much of our movies and popular culture still revolve around people failing, falling short, and then overcoming obstacles to succeed. When we're in the position where we need to apologize, our greatest obstacle is often ourselves. We fight back against those traits that hobbled us. Whether we're a politician caught in a scandal, a business executive who failed at leadership, or a spouse caught cheating in an affair, our apology serves as a request for patience to learn, space to heal, and a second chance for redemption.

Sacco herself went from being one of the world's most talked-about Internet villains to again finding success in her chosen field of public relations. As a side note, the person who first made her infamous tweet go viral, Biddle, eventually expressed some remorse for the incident. And he himself was the subject of a controversy. While writing for the now-defunct news site Gawker, Biddle sent a series of tweets denigrating video gamers. One of them—"Bring back bullying"—caused Gawker to lose several advertisers.

Biddle offered an apology.

Why Do Apologies Help?

So here's a question: Why do we ever apologize? Does it work? Is there really a benefit?

There's a tremendous amount of psychological research into apologies and how they affect both sides involved. Many of these studies characterize the players into two categories: the transgressor, or the one who did wrong, and the victim, the person wronged. Those terms are probably too general. In some cases, particularly when it comes to a reputational crisis, the word *victim* is a bit too strong. Some people have a perceived grievance—"This offends my values"—that really doesn't make them a true victim. But for the purposes of understanding how we all respond to an apology, we'll use those terms.

When we mess up and are called out for it, we become acutely aware that we've caused damage to someone and, most importantly, to ourselves. Research suggests that we, as transgressors, are most concerned with how we're viewed not only by the person we somehow wronged but also by the rest of society. According to Yale researchers Nurit Shnabel and Arie Nadler, who wrote about the dynamic in an article in 2008 in the *Journal of Personality and Social Psychology*, for a transgressor, any incident in need of apology and reconciliation "threatens one's image as moral and socially acceptable." This hits us at the heart of who we are. Though we may have only wronged a single person, we've also harmed broader society in a way that calls out for broader amends—at least in our minds.

Think of a spouse who admits to infidelity. The person most wronged is the other spouse, but the existence of the affair causes a ripple effect. Children are hurt because the affair causes a rift within the family. There are often in-laws and friends affected. (Anyone who has been through the ritual of dividing friends after a divorce, as I have, knows full well the community implications of a breakup.) If the infidelity is exposed more broadly, because of vengeful social media posts or perhaps the newsworthiness of the people involved, the affair can have farther-reaching career implications. In 2019, McDonald's Corp. CEO Steve Easterbrook lost his job when news of affairs with women at the company came to light. Same was true in the past for top executives at companies like Boeing, General Electric, and Intel. Why? Because not only do they have responsibilities to their family but also to shareholders and boards of directors who expect better behavior, particularly when workplace affairs could expose companies to workplace harassment liability and ruin trust among the rank-and-file. "Being a CEO is different," Margaret Heffernan wrote in a 2016 piece for *The Observer*. "With your special powers come special constraints. Your workforce can have affairs with coworkers, but you can't."

In fact, the more trust you're given, the bigger the impact on whom is affected. Gen. David Petraeus rose from leading the US war effort in Afghanistan to serving as director of the Central Intelligence Agency. Subsequently, it was disclosed that he had a long-term affair with author Paula Broadwell beginning in 2011, shortly after taking over the CIA. Broadwell was not a government employee, but the nature of the relationship was seen as a potential national security risk. After all, an affair has often been used in extortion attempts through history. So Petraeus was seen as betraying the public trust—which he indeed did since he ultimately pleaded guilty in 2015 to a federal misdemeanor charge of mishandling classified materials, which were discovered in his home as part of a broader FBI investigation into his affair.

Because our shortcomings often break bonds of trust—and this goes beyond extramarital affairs—it's easy to see how we might need to repair our relationships with ourselves first. An apology is necessary for reconciliation because we also need to free ourselves of the view that we have somehow lost the trust and societal acceptability we enjoyed before we perpetrated whatever necessitated the apology in the first place.

That doesn't mean forgiving ourselves before an apology. That can come later. But we do have to understand that our instinct toward apology needs to take into account our psychological requirement that we regain the trust of a community. We make amends to many, not just the individual most wronged. If we're in jail for knocking over a liquor store, the justice meted out was because of the act of robbing that store and disturbing the safety of the workers and owners. But we're imprisoned and, theoretically, work toward rehabilitation for broader societal reasons. Society doesn't want us grabbing a mask and a handgun as our job ever, ever again.

So an apology helps repair our own view of our place in society. But does it help the victims? Research pretty much agrees it does—provided the apology is delivered properly. Just as we, as transgressors, approach an apology with a need to reconcile with society, so too victims approach an apology with their own agendas. Any offense is seen as an attack on one's status and power, according to Shnabel and Nadler. And that makes sense. When you lie, cheat, steal, say something inappropriate, or fail someone in any way, it takes something away from the victim. At minimum, it breaks a bond of trust, which robs others of a worldview they had before your action. There is always some kind of victim. You take from someone else. You lie to someone else. You violate someone else's rules. No one has to apologize for a victimless crime. There's always a residual impact, and that takes away from the power, authority, or—most of all—peace of mind that the victim had.

Any apology needs to come from a place where you understand that the person most closely affected by your action needs to be compensated for that loss of status and power. Your willingness to apologize unreservedly is a step in that direction. You, in an effort to restore your place in the community, apologize in a way that gives back status and power to the victim. When done right, an apology can be a great step to repair that broader relationship. In a successful apology, "victims must restore their sense of power, whereas perpetrators must restore their public moral image," according to Shnabel and Nadler.

But it has to be done right. As we will explore later, a bad apology runs the risk of making your situation worse. As much as apologies help us personally to move on, we also have psychological barriers to apologizing effectively. Two of these are fairly obvious. According to Karina Schumann, a professor of psychology at the University of Pittsburgh who's one of the foremost researchers on the psychology around apologies, we often start with the perception that an apology won't be effective in helping us, so we just phone it in. (This literally happens when we text or email an apology rather than make the point to try to meet personally or more directly.) Second, we often fail to offer a high-quality apology because we really have low concern for the victim or the relationship that was damaged.

But Schumann's third point is most telling. We believe that an apology will somehow be a threat to our own self-image. We see it as a weakness rather than a strength. Perhaps we're embarrassed. Very often we are. An apology, after all, is an explicit admission of how we have transgressed on someone else. As we'll explore later, we have to own and understand the nature of our actions, which means reliving them in our mind even when our brains may be trying to avoid further self-damage by walling off our actions and burying them. Reliving and owning our bad behavior and mistakes is absolutely necessary, but it's also a reminder that our own personal failures are sure to be perceived as weaknesses.

History pushes us in the direction of thinking an apology makes us soft. John Wayne, the twentieth century's ultimate man's man, delivered the famous line in *She Wore a Yellow Ribbon*: "Never apologize, mister. It's a sign of weakness." That same line was requoted in more modern media, in both *Little Miss Sunshine* and the television series *NCIS*. The phrase "Never apologize, never explain" is so widespread in history it's attributed to everyone from King Charles I to Winston Churchill to Gertrude Stein.

It's all bad advice. We'll never find personal redemption unless we spend time understanding that strength comes from facing problems, not running away from them. Truly confronting our behavior is a sign of strength. As bestselling author Steven R. Covey notes, you actually cannot offer an apology from a standpoint of weakness. "It takes a great deal of character strength to apologize quickly out of one's heart rather than out of pity," Covey wrote. "A person must possess himself and have a deep sense of security in fundamental principles and values in order to genuinely apologize."

So finding that inner strength at a time when we're likely at our lowest is important for being able to genuinely deliver the right apology but also to help our own personal healing. We need to gather and muster the strength to confront both our own bad actions and the victims we left behind. There's nothing weak about facing up to your problems.

Victims see that. Most people are open to some measure of reconciliation. But because they feel that their power or worldview has been harmed, they need to see some sort of debasement from the transgressor. That act restores the power balance that's lost. Until that power balance is restored, you can't trust again. An apology helps the victim in knowing that the balance is shifting back to their own needs and values.

And then when done right, a magical transformation occurs. The restoration of balance allows the victim to actually have feelings again for the transgressor. Later, we'll talk about the role of showing empathy for the victim when we get into the nuts and bolts of an apology, but saying sorry can actually engender empathy for the victim. When we're wronged and we receive an apology, "we are then able to develop a new image of that person," wrote Beverly Engel in 2016 in *Psychology Today*. "Instead of seeing him through anger and bitterness, the person's humility and apology cause us to see him as a fallible, vulnerable human being. We see the wrongdoer as more human, more like ourselves and this moves us."

So an apology helps both the transgressor and the victim at a psychological level, which is why going beyond sorry and delivering an effective apology often works to help restore broken bonds. But there are rules, and understanding the language around hurt and healing is important before embarking on the first step of reputational repair and healing.

What Does Sorry Even Mean?

Words matter when we're owning up to our faults. But they also matter in how we plan to seek redemption after we screw up. In fact, looking at the very words that describe our apologies, our sorrow, and our attempts to reconcile with others, you can see how these words show the complexity in approaches and opportunities in making things right.

The best example is in the word *apology* itself. *Apology* comes from the Greek *apologia*, which, far from being a sign that one is sorry, actually means "mounting a defense of your position." The two most famous *Apologias* in history speak to that. The *Apology of Socrates*, as recounted by Plato, is Socrates's defense against charges that he was corrupting the minds of the youth of Athens and denying of the sanctity of the gods. Socrates defends himself against multiple attacks but to no avail. In the end he is convicted and sentenced to death. But rather than showing an instinct toward a modern apology, he goes to his death without remorse, saying, "The hour of departure has arrived, and we go our separate ways, I to die, and you to live. Which of these two is better only God knows."

Likewise, centuries later, John Henry Newman wrote the famous *Apologia Pro Vita Sua* as a defense of his abandonment of the Anglican church and conversion to Roman Catholicism. Like Socrates, the defense in his famous apology is hardly shrinking. In fact, it is designed to be unassailable as when he says confidently that "ten thousand difficulties do not make one doubt."

As a result the English word *apology* is what's known as a contranym, or a word that can mean the opposite of itself. (Think of the word *bolt*. It can mean "to lock down" or "to run away.") When we talk about a modern apology, though, we usually think of it less as a defense than a plea for forgiveness. If anything, people nowadays are (wisely) counseled not to couch apologies with any defense of their actions. That modern audiences might believe Socrates was sorry for what he taught might have him willingly reaching for a dose of hemlock all over again.

Being "sorry" has been more consistent from a word standpoint, but it too has seen an evolution and some confusion. One might think that the English words *sorry* and *sorrow* come from the same root since we often feel sadness and remorse when we are sorry, but they come from two completely different derivatives.

Etymologists say the word *sorry* comes from the same roots as the word *sore*, meaning we are pained, scabby, or covered with scars. Dwell on that a moment: When we are sorry for what we have done, how much do our feelings seem like scars? Our mistakes cause harm to others, yes, but they also do harm to ourselves. We wear our bad actions on us. That drives us being sorry.

Sorrow comes from a different word origin, meaning "grief." So traditionally, when we are sorry, we feel physical pain for our actions, and when we feel a pang of sorrow, we grieve for what our actions have done to others or for whatever we feel we have lost.

Of course, the strength of our apologies isn't going to be judged by etymologists, but it's helpful to see how humans over the years have really struggled with the idea of how best to own up to and move on from the actions that have somehow alienated themselves from the people around them. The struggle has been real for as long as humans have formed communities, and that's evident in how religions of the world have almost demanded some manner of apology and remorse. Take the Hindu concept of Prayashchit, which holds that you can rise above your bad acts by repenting for them and being redeemed.

In fact, the richness and depth to the words and philosophies around asking for forgiveness and seeking redemption, both personal and spiritual, come from religion. The most solemn holiday in Judaism is Yom Kippur, which is the ultimate lesson in how to apologize. During the Yom Kippur service, Jews around the world list their transgressions and sins, either collectively or, in some synagogues, individually and personally. They then sing the V'al Kulam: "V'al kulam eloha selichot—s'lach lanu, m'chal lanu, kaper lanu," which translates into, "For all these sins, forgiving God, forgive us, pardon us, grant us atonement."

Those are three very different words and concepts and crucial to understand even for someone preparing for a more mundane and secular apology. You can ask for forgiveness, which means you're asking for others to give up their anger, hurt, and desire for revenge for what you've done to them. But that's just one request. Good apologies seek pardon, which is a recognition that the pain caused was both lesson and punishment enough.

And then there's atonement, a word we don't use enough when we think about apologizing. Yom Kippur is known as the Day of Atonement because it again allows people to be again one with their God. To atone means exactly how it is spelled—"at one"—meaning a coming together to become "one" again. When we harm a spouse, or a child, or a coworker, we break a bond with them. We become separate. At its heart, our desire shouldn't be to simply be forgiven but to return to that bond we once had with them. We can never redeem ourselves in the eyes of the people we've wronged unless we do everything we can to again be one with them. You can't move on otherwise unless you at least make that attempt, as difficult as it might seem.

Judaism doesn't have a monopoly on this. In Catholicism, there's the great concept of contrition. The word's roots come from the Latin word for crushing and grinding stones into tiny pieces. We are crushed by our actions. Not only have you done wrong but that act has destroyed you—and you know it. Think of this in a professional context. Executives who've been outed for discriminatory or boorish behavior can't simply say they're sorry and move on. They have to show that they have felt deeply the absolute devastation their actions have had on others and themselves and own that. True contrition requires an examination of the damage we created and why. Only by searching the rubble of actions can we truly see the pieces in our work and our lives that we have to put back together.

That's also a requirement for the concept of reconciliation, which is what we're seeking for our own personal or professional redemption after a failure. Like the idea of atonement, reconciling requires reconnection. It means getting back to the time in our lives when we didn't alienate others. Being forgiven is one thing, but being trusted again is something completely different. When we seek reconciliation with coworkers, family, or stakeholders, it's a human conversation and, thus, far harder to achieve the reconciliation and redemption we seek. That's why Alexander Pope's reminder, "To err is human, to forgive, divine" resonates so much. As hard as it may seem for you to apologize for your own mistakes and errors, it's damn near God-like to be able to forgive someone. Reconciliation is a two-way street: It must be offered, *and* it must be accepted.

And then there's the concept of redemption. Again, we toss around this word without understanding the meaning of it. It comes from Latin, meaning to "buy back." We're able to take back what was once ours, ideally in the same condition that we once enjoyed. But with reputation and trust, our buyback often is more akin to a car we bought new then sold then reclaimed. Reputational and personal lapses often leave dings and chips, if not full-fledged dents. But we can substantially get back what we once had through working toward finding that redemption.

This redemption is driven by us. That's why we often talk about athletes redeeming themselves after a bad play. It's less a frame of mind than a way to act. We redeem ourselves through acts that somehow make up for what we've done wrong. In the simplest terms, if we fight with a spouse, we can attempt to redeem ourselves by perhaps buying flowers or a gift. Most of the problems we face professionally, though, are more complex and require more complex actions. If you're a CEO whose fallen short of hiring people of color, you redeem yourself and your organization not simply by agreeing to hire a more diverse staff but by creating a network and opportunities for people to help do your part to fight systemic racism. The level of your actions will dictate the success and the scope of your personal redemption.

All of this is hard work. Being open to the scars necessary to be sorry, undergoing the examination needed for true contrition, doing the work to find atonement and reconciliation with people you've alienated, and facing the uncertainty and vulnerability that comes from true redemption requires a tremendous amount of energy and effort. That's at the heart of going beyond sorry.

It's worth it, though. For one thing, without the path of owning up to your failings and repairing your relationships, you stand to never be trusted again. We live in a world that's quick to judge and can expose you and remind you of your flaws through a handful of characters typed out in a tweet. There's a social media mob ready to continue an attack on your character, hurting your personal relationships and your professional prospects. Your ability to heal the harm you created directly with the people most aggrieved will determine your ability to find redemption, atone, and thrive.

Now that we know the language of going beyond sorry, it's time to understand how we need to use our words and control our actions to own up to our mistakes and move forward.

Chapter 2

Owning It

Taking Ownership

Of all the things on his mind on the night of June 5, 1944, Gen. Dwight D. Eisenhower still took the time to sit down and write a letter.

He had already given the order for nine divisions of American and British troops to cross the English Channel and land on the beaches of Normandy. It would be the largest invasion ever attempted and obviously a huge risk. Succeed and the Allies would have a foothold in Europe and could march to Berlin and take down Adolf Hitler. Fail and the Germans would have a secure western front for years and could turn their attention on holding back the Russians.

There's a cliché that success has many fathers, but failure is an orphan, and Ike knew that. He was also comfortable with that responsibility. Ike wasn't going to do anything but own his decisions—and own the potential for his possible failure. On the night of the D-Day invasion, he sat down and wrote just a few lines:

> Our landings in the Cherbourg-Havre area have failed to gain a satisfactory foothold and I have withdrawn the troops. My decision to attack at this time and place was based upon the best information available. The troops, the air

and the Navy did all that Bravery and devotion
to duty could do. If any blame or fault attaches to
the attempt it is mine alone.

He then stuffed the note in his pocket and chain-smoked his
way through the rest of his night.

In the end, Eisenhower had nothing to apologize for. The
D-Day landing was successful, leading eventually to the fall of the
Third Reich. Also, notice Eisenhower didn't actually say he was sorry
in his preemptive letter. He simply accepts the blame and the fault.
He owns the failure. And he owns failure, and a worst-case scenario
to boot, even knowing all his planning could result in success.

If D-Day had failed, Eisenhower could have blamed a number
of factors. The weather leading up to the invasion was horrific. There
was infighting among the Allies that made coordination difficult.
Officers and troops down the line could have failed in certain aspects
of executing the plan. Yet it never even entered Eisenhower's mind to
cede an iota of responsibility to anyone other than himself. "If any
blame or fault attaches to the attempt, *it is mine alone.*"

That's leadership. It's also a great example of what it means to
own a situation. Owning the situation is often the hardest part of
apologizing and moving forward from a crisis. We often see our crisis
as a collection of circumstances, many of which are outside our control, and we decide a course of action based on addressing all those
moving parts. But that's not how others view the crisis situations we
create. They view situations from the standpoint of *who* is to blame
rather than *what* is to blame. And blame they will. Psychologists tell
us that people who are wronged or aggrieved usually turn to blame
as their first defense mechanism over the pain they feel. For the most
part, that blame is justified. To a spouse who has been the victim of
infidelity, it's never the circumstances in the marriage that caused the
crisis. It's the cheating spouse.

One of the hardest parts of owning your actions is admitting
that no matter what the other circumstances are, you have to take
responsibility for the whole situation. One of the worst apologies you
can give starts with, "I'm sorry, but you..." That doesn't fly. Most

leaders and successful people know that they must never be at the whim of circumstances but, rather, they must be the master of them.

"People are always blaming their circumstances for what they are," George Bernard Shaw wrote. "I don't believe in circumstances. The people who get on in this world are they who get up and look for the circumstances they want, and, if they can't find them, make them."

So we have to own not only our actions but also all the circumstances around them. If we say something offensive, we need to own our words but then also own all the circumstances—how we came to the thinking that what we said was wrong, how we created an environment around us where saying something like that was okay, how we failed to recognize that an audience might not like the words or sentiments we are using.

Make no mistake, if you're in a crisis where you're called upon to fix something with an apology, it's on you. We commonly refer to an apology as a *mea culpa*. That phrase actually is an admission rather than an apology. It comes from one of the most common prayers in Roman Catholicism and part of the line: *mea culpa, mea culpa, mea maxima culpa,* translates to, "Through my fault, through my fault, through my most grievous fault." While the prayer seeks forgiveness for sins, that plea for mercy only comes after the penitent admits and owns the fault. Apologies have to start with the same sense of ownership. This happened through my acts. This happened through my fault. Yes, there may have been other factors at work, but this is my life, my action, and as an owner, I am responsible.

That's what true ownership means. When we own something, it's ours, as the very word suggests: our own. When we own property, we can do what we want with it, including sharing it or selling it to others or using it as we see fit. In short, ownership means we're in control of something. When we own ourselves and our actions, the same concept applies: We are in control of ourselves. Very often, we hear people try to explain an action by saying "because of circumstances beyond my control" or "because of unforeseen circumstances," but this starts an apology or crisis statement from the standpoint that the issue itself is the problem. Not only is that person not owning the circumstances, but it suggests the circumstances themselves are beyond control.

In fact, if circumstances are truly beyond control, one wonders whether an apology is even warranted. For instance, many conferences and events were canceled as a result of 2020's COVID-19 outbreak. Those cancellations caused many bands, artists, and businesses to refund tickets and fees. In many cases, businesses communicated with their audiences in the form of an apology: "Because of circumstances beyond our control and out of an abundance of caution, we are sorry to say we are canceling our tour." But here, saying sorry isn't necessary. People, many of whom were home anyway because of worldwide lockdowns, certainly knew the circumstances and weren't seeking an apology. There was nothing to own in that case and no reason to be sorry.

Buddhists understand the concept of ownership of their lives very well. In fact, Buddhist teaching holds that our happiness is a direct result of our own actions. The last of Buddha's "five reminders" is "I am the owner of my actions, heir to my actions, born of my actions, related through my actions, and have my actions as my arbitrator. Whatever I do, for good or for evil, to that will I fall heir."

One of the best examples of ownership from what could have been a major and career-killing event was when British actor Hugh Grant was arrested for "lewd conduct" with a prostitute in Los Angeles in 1995. Grant was a well-respected and well-loved star and also in a very public and committed relationship with actress Elizabeth Hurley. The arrest and famous mugshot (where Grant's face clearly showed he wanted to be in front of any other camera than that particular one) were major news.

Rather than making denials or stepping around the issue, Grant's approach was refreshingly direct. In a public statement issued the very next day after the arrest, he said, "Last night, I did something completely insane. I have hurt people I love and embarrassed people I work with. For both things I am more sorry than I can ever possibly say."

There was no attempt to couch his act. It was, after all, a dumb move, one where his libido got the better part of his judgment. For him, it was insane and apparently out of character. And he recognized that went beyond simple personal embarrassment to an act that created real damage to his relationships. He was sorry for that and said so—unreservedly.

If that wasn't an example of clear ownership, he went on *The Tonight Show with Jay Leno* soon after and somehow found a way to take even more responsibility. "The thing is," he told Leno, "people give me tons of ideas on this one. I keep reading new, you know, psychological theories and stuff like that, that I was under pressure or I was overtired or I was lonely or I fell down the stairs when I was a child or whatever. But I think that would be bollocks to hide behind something like that. I think you know in life pretty much what's a good thing to do and what's a bad thing, and I did a bad thing. There you have it."

Grant knew ownership has no room for excuses, and the result of his apology was an outpouring of forgiveness, pardon, and support.

Avoiding Denial

Notice at no point—even though there were clear legal ramifications—did Grant deny what he had done. You cannot own the situation if you don't admit you've done something wrong. If you aren't at fault, that's another matter entirely, but very often we deny, deny, deny even when we are at fault. There's a scene in the 1967 classic *A Guide to the Married Man* where Joey Bishop, caught by his wife *in flagrante delicto* with a mistress, simply denies that his lover is even in the room. "What girl?" he asks casually while they both casually get dressed again. By the time the girl walks out, his wife ends up believing him. The immoral moral of that scene? Deny. Deny. Deny.

It works in schtick but not in real life. While, when faced with a crisis, our first instinct might be to deny all wrongdoing, that's rarely a path to being able to reclaim your reputation.

The most famous false denial probably came when President Bill Clinton was confronted with allegations that he had sex with intern Monica Lewinsky in the Oval Office in the late 1990s. "But

I want to say one thing to the American people," he told reporters when asked about the allegations. "I want you to listen to me. I'm going to say this again: I did not have sexual relations with that woman, Miss Lewinsky. I never told anybody to lie, not a single time, never. These allegations are false. And I need to go back to work for the American people."

Of course, history showed this denial was false. From a reputational standpoint, it was among the worst ways to handle the situation because in the end, the denial compounded and actually amplified the crisis. In the end, Clinton's impeachment was about perjury—lying under oath—which made his credibility, rather than his personal behavior, more of the issue. His initial denial certainly didn't help.

What was interesting about President Clinton's blanket denial was that Washington is known as the place where politicians parse words to make it seem that they are denying something when they really aren't—an approach legendary *Washington Post* editor Ben Bradlee coined a "nondenial denial." In some cases, this kind of denial can look even worse than a simple lie. In 2005, during Congressional hearings about the use of steroids in Major League Baseball, slugger Mark McGuire was asked over and over again by a wide range of congresspeople whether he indeed used steroids. Repeatedly, he kept saying, "I'm not here to talk about the past." He said it so much that it almost because a joke and has become one of the most famous examples of an ineffective evasion.

Not only was McGuire denying his actions, but he may also have been in denial. Sigmund Freud defined denial as "knowing but not knowing." Essentially, when faced with an external situation that we find too much to handle, our minds try their damnedest to make the problem just go away. It's a defensive mechanism our brains employ to protect us from things that are most unpleasant. Freud introduced three different types of denial: simple denial, minimization, and projection. All of them are very common responses that get in our way of taking ownership of our crisis, so it's worth exploring each.

Simple denial is what the term implies: simply not believing in reality. We all suffer from simple denial, and some psychologists argue it permeates our life. In his seminal (and Pulitzer Prize-winning) book *The Denial of Death,* cultural anthropologist Ernest Becker took Freud's work further, saying our entire human civilization is built around tricking ourselves into thinking we are immortal. Death just can't exist because acknowledging it takes away meaning from life and leads to conditions like depression. "What does it mean to be a self-conscious animal?" Ernst wrote. "The idea is ludicrous, if it is not monstrous. It means to know that one is food for worms. This is the terror: to have emerged from nothing, to have a name, consciousness of self, deep inner feelings, an excruciating inner yearning for life and self-expression and with all this yet to die. It seems like a hoax, which is why one type of cultural man rebels openly against the idea of God. What kind of deity would create such a complex and fancy worm food?" Being worm food is clearly something worth denying.

From an apology standpoint, a simple denial is what we often see when someone is accused of a crime. It is encapsulated in the "not guilty" plea invariably issued in a first court appearance. It's celebrated in rapper Shaggy's 2001 hit "It Wasn't Me," which contains the admonition, "To be a true player you have to know how to play; / If she say a night, convince her say a day" and then reinforces that even in the most compromised positions, a simple denial works:

> But she caught me on the counter (It wasn't me)
> Saw me bangin' on the sofa (It wasn't me)
> I even had her in the shower (It wasn't me)
> She even caught me on camera (It wasn't me)

For the record, it makes for a good song, but a lousy approach.

The second kind of denial Freud identified was minimization. Here we trigger a defense that makes our offense seem less important or impactful. If, after you've wronged someone, you immediately tell them that it's no big deal, you're practicing minimization. Such minimization can have disastrous consequences. In 2009, hundreds of owners of Toyota cars complained that without warning, their cars suddenly accelerated, causing accidents and injuries. Toyota, rather than act aggressively on what could have been a major and deadly manufacturing flaw, blamed the sudden acceleration on floor mats and driver error, thus minimizing the issue. Even as more evidence emerged, Toyota repeatedly downplayed the problems, blaming an occasional "sticky pedal."

It wasn't a small problem but rather a very big deal, prompting Toyota eventually to recall nine million of its cars, replacing the pedals and installing new braking software. What's more, because Toyota chose to minimize the issue, it was forced to admit federal charges that the company misled consumers and made deceptive statements about the problem. Such minimization led Toyota to pay $1.2 billion to settle the charges—the largest penalty for an automaker in US history at the time.

Addicts are well-known for minimization. Anyone who has been hurt by someone's addiction knows that when confronted, they very often say their drinking or drug use is no big deal or is being blown out of proportion. It's the easiest way to deny that a problem exists. Conversely, alcohol or drugs are often used as a way to minimize the bad behavior people engage in, often obscuring deeper issues that should be at the heart of a subsequent apology.

The last kind of denial Freud identified was projection. Projection is taking out our own shortcomings and ascribing them to people around us. We hide from our own transgressions and misdeeds by seeing those same acts or traits in others around us. By sharing the blame, we don't have to feel guilty on our own. We can also justify our bad behavior by suggesting that "everybody does it" even if they don't.

Projection happens frequently in infidelity. The partner having an affair with someone else often feels jealous that their own partner too is being unfaithful—even in the absence of evidence. Researchers Angela Neal and Edward Lemay looked at this phenomenon in 2017 and found that it was an absolute denial-based defense mechanism. It's easier for us to direct anger at the perception that we are being cheated on than to face the consequences of our own infidelity. And we sometimes make the perceived affair look even worse than our own. As the researchers concluded, "People who are themselves attracted to alternative partners may exaggerate their partner's extradyadic attraction as a way of alleviating guilt or justifying their own attraction to others."

One of the worst examples of projection came from one of the biggest financial criminals in history: Bernard Madoff. Madoff was a giant of Wall Street, well-known and well-respected and with a client list that included celebrities like Kevin Bacon on down to regular folks who entrusted him with their nest eggs. Madoff was known for some of the best returns on Wall Street. He was also a leader for the broader financial community, serving in various capacities in financial trade organizations and sitting on several philanthropic boards.

Trouble was, Madoff wasn't actually investing anything. Through a scheme involving falsified statements and a marketing approach that always ensured incoming cash from investors, Madoff was able to inflate the size of people's portfolios for decades. As long as new money came in and clients were slow to make withdrawals, all of his clients believed Madoff was helping them outperform the market.

Circumstances began to unravel for Madoff in 2008 amid the financial crisis when nervous investors decided they would rather keep their money in cash than invest it in a consistently falling market. Madoff watched as investors asked for their money back. Just before Christmas in 2008, Madoff told his sons Mark and Andrew, who worked at the business, that the nation's financial crisis prompted him to want to make multimillion-dollar bonus payments to his staff. The sons were suspicious and confronted him, at which point Madoff admitted the business was a fraud. His own sons turned him in.

In the end, Madoff pled guilty to all the charges prosecutors brought against him—a sure sign of the psychological burden keeping up appearances had inflicted on him. He was sentenced to 150 years in prison with an agreement to pay $7.4 billion in restitution (which, clearly, he didn't have). He refused to cooperate with prosecutors, claiming it was his fraud alone in a bid to protect his coconspirators. While he made an apology at his sentencing, it was somewhat perfunctory for someone who had admitted to the greatest Ponzi scheme in American history. "I have left a legacy of shame, as some of my victims have pointed out, to my family and my grandchildren," Madoff said in court. "This is something I will live in for the rest of my life. I'm sorry. I know that doesn't help you."

Madoff, though, would later give an interview with *New York Magazine* that showed signs of simple denial but was a true master class in projection. Speaking to journalist Steve Fishman in 2011, Madoff said, "I'm not the kind of person I'm being portrayed as," emphasizing, "I am a good person."

He wasn't all to blame, he said. In fact, he said, there were a number of people who drove him to this—namely all the people around him socially. "We made a very nice living," Madoff told Fishman. "I didn't need the investment-advisory business. I took it on and got myself involved in it, but if you think I woke up one morning and said, 'Well, listen, I need to be able to buy a boat and a plane, and this is what I'm going to do,' that's wrong. I had more than enough money to support my lifestyle and my family's lifestyle. I allowed myself to be talked into something, and that's my fault. I thought I could extricate myself after a short period of time. But I just couldn't."

Then there were the major banks, which he said were just as complicit because they never asked him any questions and were just as driven by greed as he was. "These banks and these funds had to know there were problems," Madoff said. "I wouldn't give them any facts, like how much volume I was doing. I was not willing to have them come up and do the due diligence that they wanted. I absolutely refused to do it. I said, 'You don't like it, take your money out,' which of course they never did."

He also had the gall to blame his clients—the ones whose nest eggs he obliterated—citing their own greed. "They were all told by me, 'Don't invest any more money than you could afford to lose,'" Madoff said. "'This is the stock market. There's always stuff that can happen. Brokerage firms can fail. I could go crazy and do something stupid. If you want a [safe thing], put your money in government bonds.' So everybody understood this. Everyone was greedy. I just went along."

So much for Madoff being sorry. Clearly, you can't own what you did wrong if you blame everyone around you.

Examining Our Conscience

True ownership over an issue, your words or actions really demands an examination of conscience. Conscience is one of those concepts that exists in several realms of our life. It has connotations across philosophy, religion, and psychology. It's tremendously complex. For centuries, people have tried to define what makes us explore our actions and feelings. Our conscience guides our decisions, allowing us to judge them in terms like right or wrong. But right or wrong isn't black and white. Over the years, saints, philosophers, and psychiatrists have argued over whether our consciences are defined by our environment, our communities, or simply an external sense of what God expects of us. For the purposes of going beyond sorry, a cage match between Thomas Aquinas and Immanuel Kant wouldn't be helpful, but it's important to know that conscience—no matter where it is derived—is an important yardstick. At its heart, it's a moral judgment of our actions based on an examination of whether we did a right or wrong thing. Kant himself famously wrote that we have a duty to "know (scrutinize, fathom) yourself, not in terms of your natural perfection (your fitness or unfitness for all sorts of discretionary or even commanded ends) but rather in terms of your moral perfection in relation to your duty. That is, know your heart—whether it is good or evil, whether the source of your actions is pure or impure, and what can be imputed to you as belonging originally to the substance of a human being or as derived (acquired or developed) and belonging to your moral condition."

This use of conscience in knowing right or wrong is essential for our individual self-examination in order to own our actions. For some, it's easy. Conscience often leads to the guilt of our actions, which makes understanding easier. We carry the burden of the wrongs we've done, so when we are truly connected to our conscience and we acknowledge our misbehavior, we actually use conscience as a way to offer us relief. After all, it's hard to consciously carry around the wrong we've done. As Protestant theologian John Calvin put it, "The torture of a bad conscience is the hell of a living soul."

But for others, truly understanding what we've done wrong so that we can own it and go beyond sorry is trickier. Here, religion can show a good example of that process even if we're dealing with secular issues. (You don't have to be religious to understand the motivations and the pathway.) In Roman Catholicism, an examination of conscience is a necessary step before seeking the Sacrament of Reconciliation or the forgiveness of your sins. These examinations are usually in the form of questions. At their most basic, we ask ourselves, "What did I do wrong?" You need the self-knowledge of your transgression before you can ever own it to deliver an effective apology.

Here, you should be as specific as possible. Instead of saying you told lies, explore specifically the lies you told. If you said something that offended someone else, what was at the heart of the offense? What role did you have in causing harm?

A very public examination of conscience happened in the summer of 2020 after the shooting death by a Minneapolis policeman of George Floyd. As people in cities across America took to the streets to protest in the nascent days of what became known as the Black Lives Matter movement, many families and businesses came together to explore their own understanding of systemic racism. In many corporate boardrooms, there was a reckoning of corporate conscience to ask why Blacks were so historically underrepresented in the American workforce and why there were even fewer Blacks in executive leadership positions and in the very boardrooms taking on the issue. Many companies increased spending, attention, and resources on diversity and inclusion efforts, but the immediate action was supported by real discussions about why change hadn't happened sooner.

In fact, that examination of conscience led to a change in thinking. When Wells Fargo CEO John Scharf in June 2020 wanted to address the bank's own perceived lack of diversity, he wrote in an internal memo, "While it might sound like an excuse, the unfortunate reality is that there is a very limited pool of Black talent to recruit from." Critics pounced on this, saying that the statement both minimized the tremendous amount of Black talent in the workforce but also failed to acknowledge that companies like Wells Fargo had a responsibility to create a network to build a Black workforce—which it, like other corporations, had failed to do, feeding the cycle of racism.

Scharf found himself having to apologize for what he characterized as "an insensitive comment reflecting my own unconscious bias." "There are many talented diverse individuals working at Wells Fargo and throughout the financial services industry and I never meant to imply otherwise," he wrote. "It's clear to me that, across the industry, we have not done enough to improve diversity, especially at senior leadership levels. And there is no question Wells Fargo has to make meaningful progress to increase diverse representation."

Like the examination around racism nationally, a personal examination of conscience is rarely pleasant. In many ways, it forces us to look upon the worst that we have done. Invariably, whatever act you committed that has brought you to the need to go beyond sorry has somehow violated a norm. You may have done something illegal. In that case, you have consequences to face but also a reckoning leading up to the punishment. In court cases, that reckoning is often in the form of evidence and testimony. We can help guide our own examination by following the words and details that police and prosecutors use to try to convict us. In this case, an examination of conscience could take the form of understanding the motivations behind every action and every harm that led us to this place.

Most times, we don't face a legal crisis but rather one where we violated a moral or societal norm. In this case, an examination of conscience has to include a full understanding of what that norm was, how our actions were contrary to it, whom our actions harmed, and what motivated us to take the action we did.

This can be scary stuff. Despite all the rhetoric about cancel culture and the rancor one finds on social media, people are not equipped to focus on the worst in others. It can be emotionally draining. Friedrich Nietzsche warned about this, quite famously, when he wrote, "Whoever fights monsters should see to it that in the process he does not become a monster. And if you gaze long enough into an abyss, the abyss will gaze back into you." This is far worse when the abyss is within us. Our personal reckoning, our deep dive into conscience, can often lead to places we don't want to see. There are pockets of our lives we hide away. There are bad thoughts or traits we willfully ignore. So many times, when we make a mistake, our first reaction is, "I can't believe I did that." We disbelieve the wrongheadedness of our actions because we actually don't think we are capable of doing such wrong. "What was I thinking?" Well, in many cases, we aren't thinking. We are simply doing. And we are doing something that comes in a horrifically natural way. That demands an examination of conscience.

Here is an important caveat: When we truly live with the wrongs we've committed, the temptation is to hate ourselves. Feelings of self-loathing can be dangerous. After all, depression is often defined as anger turned inward. That self-loathing might cause us to want to punish ourselves for our actions. This could lead to substance abuse. It's certainly common for someone involved in a major crisis to grab a big bottle of Tito's vodka and lock themselves away. People who can trace their bad behavior to an addiction often find them trying to run away from their situation by getting even more high or impaired. Worst of all, feelings of self-anger and disappointment can, in some people, engender feelings of suicide, "taking the easy way out" as they say. All these feelings demand professional help. Seek it. It's hard to remember in times of true crisis that we're actually not alone. Find help. In fact, having someone guide you through your own examination of conscience often makes the process easier. In our darkest times, we suffer through a lack of perspective. Other people around us, particularly trained professionals, can help provide that.

As tough as that self-exploration can be, though, it's a necessary component of owning our actions. We cannot hope to recover from a crisis if we don't truly own what we've done. It will help us understand what we did wrong. It will help us understand specifically how our actions or behavior hurt others. It will put us in a genuine place to seek forgiveness and reconciliation with communities we've harmed. And most importantly, that ownership will allow us to gain deep knowledge of ourselves in a way that will put us on a path to prevent us from ever going astray again. That's the basis of going beyond sorry.

Chapter 3

Finding the Right Words

When I was a young reporter in my first newsroom in Trenton, New Jersey, in the 1990s, some of my colleagues played a little game. They would bet whether they could somehow get a specific obscure word to fit well into a story—and hardest of all, get it past the sharp-eyed copy editors who were always looking to ensure that stories were both factual and readable. One day, the word was *Naugahyde*, that awful faux leather common in couches. (How we determined these words I don't quite recall, though beer was no doubt involved.) For some reason, the editors that day were on to us, and story by story, they duly deleted every instance they found. A colleague, though, was determined to find a way to get Naugahyde into print. He was talking on the phone to a colorful police captain about an arrest, and the captain must have said that the suspect had given them a particularly fake alibi. My colleague asked, "Would you say the guy's story was as fake as Naugahyde?"

The captain, likely confused, said sure. "Then say it," my colleague said.

He did. And *voila*, a quote by a Trenton police captain found its way into print: "His story was as fake as Naugahyde." No way an editor could ever remove a direct quote like that. It was just too good.

That anecdote makes for a great story, but it's awful practice because it was so contrived. The language was as fake as Naugahyde. When going beyond sorry, our words have to fit our story. They have to be genuine. Particularly when we are trying to make amends and seek forgiveness and redemption, we have to mean what we say, or else people won't believe us.

When clients come to me now and ask them to write out what they should say, I always start with a conversation. I want to hear what they *want* to say rather than what they *think they should* say. And I want to hear it in their own words. You aren't performing an apology. You're offering one. As such, there's no great oration or script to use that will automatically make everything right. In fact, if you used someone else's script, you are using someone else's words, and those words can't ever capture the feeling and sentiment deep in your own heart that you have a duty to deliver if you want to go beyond sorry.

We often fall into the trap of trying to find the perfect words instead of the right ones. That's always the wrong approach because we aren't perfect. No one is. Because of this, a search for perfection is always a trap. The desire for perfection is almost always a symptom of another failing of ours rather than a solution. For instance, one of the biggest issues facing business executives is something called Impostor Syndrome. Impostor Syndrome is a fear, as we move up in the world, that somehow, somewhere, someone will find out that we don't deserve the position, the marriage, or the success we're enjoying. At some point, we fear that a decision we make or a phrase we utter will somehow cause others to question our own abilities. Very often, the higher-achieving we are, the worse the syndrome. It can manifest itself in many ways.

I once did a media training session with a high-ranking woman on Wall Street. In natural conversation, she came across as smart, engaging, insightful, and fearless. When she was in front of a camera, she froze, stumbling through answers and trying to rifle through pages of notes she brought with her as a crutch. The effect was that this successful business leader seemed unprepared on camera.

As we explored how she could perform for the cameras better, I asked her directly why she was so scared. "I know that people I grew up with and even people I work with don't think I deserve the job I have," she admitted. We talked about this for around an hour, and instead of focusing on some of the technical aspects of a great media appearance, we talked about trusting herself and her instincts. We talked about instances where she inspired others to action. We talked about her personal and professional journey. I told her to remind herself, before every interview and media, that she deserved everything she had. She should say "I belong here" before any media appearance or meeting. Almost immediately, her demeanor on television changed. By simply reminding herself that she belonged there, any reservations fell to the wayside. Instead of relying on her notes, she was relying on the strength of her mind and insight. Today, she's CEO of her own firm.

Personal or professional crises that lead us to seek forgiveness often exacerbate issues like Impostor Syndrome. We feel that our own shortcomings or inadequacies doomed us to our problems. Our failure was preordained. If we had just been more careful to hide our true selves, we probably could have carried on with our personal con longer. We think, wrongly, that acting in the perfect way would have protected us.

That is simply not true. As Brene Brown wrote in her fantastic book, *Daring Greatly: How the Courage to Be Vulnerable Transforms the Way We Live, Love, Parent, and Lead*, "Perfectionism is not self-improvement. Perfectionism is, at its core, about trying to earn approval... Healthy striving is self-focused. Perfectionism is a hustle."

This is true not only in our actions but also in the words we require to go beyond sorry. If the words don't come from you, you will fail. You have to believe them. You have to own them. Trouble is, there's a booming business around vocabulary. It's a racket, with dozens of companies selling apps or programs to get you to learn and use bigger and better words as if that will make you somehow seem smarter. A few years back, I remember hearing a radio commercial that started with something akin to, "Like it or not, people judge you by the words you use." I worked with an anchor in television who had a word-a-day calendar and tried to incorporate one of those words into her broadcasts every day. All of that effort, though, to pick a better word takes you further away from finding the right word, which is one you would naturally say and, more importantly, one that will resonate with the person or audience you transgressed.

It's about being genuine. There's an interesting link between the word *genuine* and the concept of ownership that we discussed in the previous chapter. The Latin etymology of the word comes from the word *genu*, which actually means "knee." Why? Well, the term was used to acknowledge paternity of a child. Ancient Romans put a baby on their knee to acknowledge that the child truly belonged to them and was accepted. That later became a synonym in English for being natural, right, or proper. But the word meant you took ownership of your brood, so it's easy to see how being genuine in our apologies requires taking ownership of your actions.

When you are genuine in your sentiment, you need to be genuine in your words. It's tempting in times of crisis to try to not be yourself. After all, after the event—and particularly following your examination of conscience—you probably have anger toward yourself. It was yourself that got you into your mess. But you can't follow someone else's script. In fact, people can always tell when you're using someone else's words.

In the United Kingdom, there's a wonderful ritual when a new Parliament is formed. The monarch rides to Westminster and summons both houses of Parliament to the House of Lords. The duty falls to King Charles III now, but no one did it more or better than the late Queen Elizabeth II, who was known for the perfect delivery of "the Queen's Speech." Those speeches laid out the priorities for the incoming government, listing the laws that would be debated in the coming months. Though it was called her speech, the queen had almost nothing to do with it. She didn't write it. Rather, the party in power did and still does. Those speeches lay out the prime minister's priorities, and as a result, they are delivered in a plain, dispassionate way. Queen Elizabeth II excelled in dispassion, carefully ensuring her elocution never tipped whether she agreed with what she read or not.

You're not the queen, so you should care more about what you're saying. At least you need to care, or no one will believe you. Just as you've owned your actions, you also have to own your apology. There's no shortcut, no matter how hard you look for one. There's the old saying—attributed to folks like Groucho Marx and Jack Benny, but really penned by French novelist Jean Giraudoux—that "the secret to success is sincerity. Once you've learned to fake that, you've got it made." That approach doesn't work. People will see through that. A lack of sincerity, a lack of presenting your genuine self with genuine words of an apology, runs the risk of compounding the harm you've done, seeming as though you're taking the situation seriously or not caring enough to make things right. Be genuine in your apology, or risk falling further behind.

Framework over Formula

Since the words have to come from you, there can't be a script. There's not a bagful of "right" words you must use. Nor is there really a formula for the right apology. But there is a framework to use to help guide your word selection.

One of the most popular research papers about the elements of an apology came from Roy Lewicki and Robert Yount of the Ohio State University and Beth Polin of Eastern Kentucky University. Writing in the journal *Negotiation and Conflict Management Research* in 2016, the authors surveyed how more than 750 people reacted to the words delivered in apologies. Through that effort, they determined there are six components to an effective apology. They are as follows:

1. An expression of regret
2. An explanation of what went wrong
3. Acknowledgment of responsibility
4. A declaration of repentance
5. An offer of repair
6. A request for forgiveness

So in the most generic way possible, an apology can look like this:

> I'm sorry for what I did to you. I wasn't
> thinking clearly, but that is no excuse. This is all
> on me. I will work on my deficiencies, and I will
> do whatever I have to do to fix this. Please forgive
> me.

As we look at those words, I'm sure we've all delivered some form of that in our lives. In fact, as we've matured, in life and in business, we've most likely used some variation of this. Invariably, we've started with some form of regret. We've been defaulting to "I'm sorry" since the first time, as children, we did something wrong. While we want to move beyond sorry, there is nothing wrong with saying "I'm sorry," as our opening words. There's nothing wrong with saying that in the last line either (order here may matter, but we'll get to that in a second).

We sometimes want to be a bit more elaborate with the expression of regret, lobbing in the adverbs and adjectives to let people know that not only are we sorry but we are "really, really sorry," and we "most humbly apologize." The more verbal modifiers you add, the less credible you are. We do this in other conversations too, and it never works. People who are trying to convince someone else of something say, "To tell you the truth..." but rather than making that statement more credible, it can sow doubt: Does that mean that everything else you've said thus far has been a lie? So when you say you're "really sorry," does that mean that other words you use are fake? It isn't just semantics. Depending on the circumstance, the person whom you transgressed may be watching every word, looking for a loophole you're trying to use to avoid true responsibility. Saying "I'm sorry" is simple, provided it comes naturally. Other words, like *regret*, can also be appropriate, but they have to come natural to your own voice.

The same guidance holds when you try to explain what you did wrong. This element demands plain language. If you own your actions and have examined what caused you to do wrong, this should be one of the easier elements of your apology. The explanation of what you did wrong should never be an attempt to explain yourself or find an excuse. As Benjamin Franklin warned, "Never ruin apology with an excuse." In fact, most real transgressions are inexcusable. If they weren't, then you can give an explanation rather than an apology. Take this as your chance to just lay out what you believe you did wrong that caused the harm. That helps show the person you transgressed that you actually know what you did, and you know it was wrong. In fact, it creates a level playing field for being able to move on with someone. Your explanation of what you did wrong allows for some sense of agreement with the transgressed. It gives the other party the chance to check your work. It forms the basis for the other elements, particularly gaining credibility for your path toward redemption and reconciliation. Be direct. Be to the point. And be accurate. "I know I did this…" Don't overdo it, either. Sometimes we talk too much, and the explanation of our actions lends itself to long stories. Avoid that trap. If someone asks you what time it is, don't tell them the history of Switzerland.

Our acknowledgment of responsibility is the final outcome of our work in owning our bad behavior or crisis. If you took the time to examine your actions and yourself and own the situation, you can simply say that. Again, there are always others you could be tempted to blame for what happened. Don't do that. It always comes across as an abrogation of responsibility.

At one of several drug-addled low points in singer Johnny Cash's career, he provided an example of how not to take responsibility when you clearly should. In June 1965, Cash was camping along Sespe Creek in Los Padres National Forest when his camper truck got stuck. He gunned the engine to try to free the truck, which led to a gas spill and sparks, which started a fire. In the end, Cash's fire caused 508 acres of federal parkland to burn. The fire killed forty-nine of the fifty-three federally protected California condors. Naturally, the government made a federal case out of the issue.

Rather than be contrite and own the situation, he (no doubt with the encouragement of amphetamines) decided to be very specific about where responsibility lay. When a federal judge asked him if he started the fire, he said, "No, my truck did, and it's dead, so you can't question it."

When asked about the condors, he said, "You mean those big yellow buzzards?"

"Yes, Mr. Cash," the judge replied, "those yellow buzzards."

"I don't give a damn about your yellow buzzards," Cash answered. "Why should I care?" The judge ordered Cash to pay $82,000 in restitution.

After taking responsibility, according to Lewicki, Yount, and Polin, we should move on to the declaration of repentance. The declaration of repentance flows easily once you take responsibility. It's an act that's a bridge from the past to the future. You know what you did was wrong, but you promise to take action to ensure that you're never going to do it again. The concept of repentance typically has a religious connotation. We think of street-corner prophets holding signs and yelling to us, "Repent! The kingdom of the Lord is at hand!" Indeed, the word's derivation and usage are quite biblical. Repentance has roots in Hebrew, where we are supposed to feel sorrow about what we've done wrong and return to the right path. In Greek, the word for *repent* is *metanoia*, which means to change one's mind and think differently.

Interestingly, a lot of religious traditions don't just call for being sorry but want repentance. In Judaism, the Babylonian Talmud makes clear that repentance doesn't just heal the person seeking forgiveness but everyone around her: "Great is repentance, for it brings healing to the world," the rabbinical text reads. "When an individual repents, he is forgiven, and the entire world with him."

Early Christianity was largely based on the concept of repentance. In fact, the nascent movement's leaders made it their central talking point. Both Peter and Paul, who had their differences in the direction of the movement, agreed and preached repeatedly at the need for people to repent for their sins.

Islam has a similar word: *tawbah*. Akin to the Hebrew, it means "to turn away" and go in another direction. And that's the point: Repentance requires certain knowledge. It starts with the knowledge that your action was wrong. It then requires you to turn away from that path and follow a new one. It's a rerouting of your moral and ethical GPS. The route you've taken before led you to a bad outcome. You hurt someone, so much so that you need to make amends. Repentance is an acknowledgment that you know what you did and you won't do it again.

So what do those words look like? Well, very simply, your expression of responsibility should have created a clear understanding that you know what you did to screw up. The trick is telling someone how you plan to behave in the future and—most importantly—why.

Let's say you posted something on social media that offended people to the point where it threatened your job. You can publicly acknowledge that your post was wrong. But people need to hear that they will never see anything like that again. But they won't just take your word for it. You also have to express why you are changing your thinking: "My previous post was offensive, and I'm sorry. I commit to being more careful not only in my words but also in my thought process. This never should have happened, and I will do the work to ensure it never happens again."

Next comes the offer of repair. This is most easily conceptualized when our harm has caused physical damage. When you hit a baseball through a neighbor's window, they no doubt appreciate that you are sorry for what was clearly a mistake, but they are most likely to forgive if you promise to not play ball in their yard again *and* you offer to pay for a new window. If you are apologizing after your conviction for a crime, your offer to repair starts with paying restitution, but it can also go beyond that to addressing the emotional or societal impact of what we did. We should work to repair every harm. Reparation is healing. While we feel the pain of what our actions have broken, both sides can find some semblance of solace in the offer to fix it.

Very often, we say something in our apologies along the lines of "I will do anything to make this right." That kind of hyperbole isn't helpful. In fact, it's not even an offer. Offers must be very specific and achievable. For instance, saying you'll do anything to repair the broken trust after being caught in an affair makes your partner the one to choose your path. Given how devastated your partner is at the moment he or she found out about the infidelity, that's not the time to ask the aggrieved partner what they want you to do. Rather, you should offer concrete steps: You will immediately end the affair. You will enter couple's counseling. You will be open and honest with yourself and your partner about what led to going down the path of cheating in the first place. Those are actual, concrete offers of repair.

Offers to repair deep emotional hurt might be rejected. Accepting repair might come too close to indicating a willingness on the other party to forgive. As we'll explore in a later chapter, you should never expect forgiveness. But you have to make the offer to try to make some restitution. Then you can at least *ask* for forgiveness.

There aren't a lot of word choices when it comes to asking for forgiveness. And there don't need to be. Simply asking someone to please forgive you is enough. We sometimes think that begging or pleading will somehow add weight to the acceptance of our apology and the granting of the gift of forgiveness. Truth is, this isn't the time for melodrama or hyperbole. It's a time for the plainest speaking, the rawest of your emotions becoming real through your words.

Interestingly, while Lewicki, Yount, and Polin talked about these six elements, the authors noted that not all of them were created equal. The research determined that the acknowledgment of responsibility was considered the most important component of an apology. Second was the offer of repair.

This makes sense. Both are probably the most important pathways to provide near-term healing. Think about it from the point of view of the person you've wronged. They are hurt. They are grieving. They are distrustful. They want answers, and they want a fix. Naturally, they blame you for the problem. (They aren't wrong.) But they want you to take responsibility for it. They want you to own it. That's why all the work you've done in owning your faults was so important. If you truly own it, you can convincingly take responsibility. The people you've offended or hurt don't want excuses. They don't want denials. They want to know that you know what you have done and that you take full ownership of that.

The fact that after ownership, people wanted an offer of repair is a gift. It means that most people do want you to try to repair the harm you've done. It might be easier for a full break. It might be easier to just walk away from someone who hurts you, offends you, or lets you down, but this research shows people want a path toward repair. That is an opening, a way forward to go beyond sorry and attempt to restore the bond of trust you lost with colleagues, friends, and family.

Earlier, when we explored the six elements of an apology, we listed them in order. But based on a deeper understanding of what resonates, it might be better to start with what works first. Recall our generic apology:

> I'm sorry for what I did to you. I wasn't thinking clearly, but that is no excuse. This is all on me. I will work on my deficiencies, and I will do whatever I have to do to fix this. Please forgive me.

In your own words, try starting with the ownership issue and follow with your offer of repair:

> I hurt you and I own that. That was my fault alone. I will do the work needed to fix this. I've learned so much in such a short time about how my actions were so harmful, and I commit to never going down this path again. I am sorry. Please forgive me.

If this was a lapse by a business, a leader can adjust it to take responsibility on behalf of an organization:

> We let down our customers and shareholders, and that's on me as CEO. We will do the work internally to restore your trust. I can assure

you this will never happen again. I am sorry.
Please give us another chance.

Notice that in all these examples, the request for forgiveness is last. It's also last on the list of what's important to people who have been wronged. They don't care that you want forgiveness. Forgiveness is last on their minds at the point when you're making an apology. Forgiveness, as we'll explore in a later chapter, is the product of the work you do, not the words you say. So as a result, never lead an apology with a request for forgiveness. You aren't in a position to make demands.

Speaking with Empathy

As you choose your words, put yourself in the shoes of the listeners. You need to think about not only what you want to say but also how those people you've wronged will hear it. That takes empathy. Empathy is one of those words that's often misused. Empathy is truly getting inside the head and heart of someone else to the point where you can actually feel what they're feeling. That's a tall order, particularly when you're not making a personal one-on-one apology but rather laying bare your faults to a wider audience. But it's essential to the apology itself.

First, remember that empathy isn't sympathy. Both have Greek roots in *pathos*, meaning feeling. But the prefixes make all the difference. Empathy is a feeling *within* the other person. Sympathy is feeling *along with* another person. Clearly, the people you've wronged don't need—nor want—your sympathy. They can get that from someone who didn't hurt them in the first place. Nor do they want or need your empathy. But you need to conjure empathy if for no other reason than to ensure that the words of your apology don't fall flat.

We express empathy at the most basic level with phrases like "I feel your pain," and that's a good start. While much of the work of going beyond sorry has centered on the work you need to do within yourself, that's all meaningless unless you at least try to figure out the harm you've done. Once you've owned your actions, it helps to try to imagine, in a very specific way, the feelings and emotions your actions engendered.

Let's look at hypothetical and all-too-common crime: a house break-in. The thief breaks in, steals items, and leaves. From the thief's perspective, the harm he did was to take someone else's property and try to profit from it, perhaps leaving behind some physical damage along the way. If he is caught and wants to apologize, he may say, "I'm sorry I stole your TV" or "I'm sorry I broke your window and knocked over furniture when I broke into your house." But chances are good the homeowner herself doesn't care about that aspect of the crime. A break-in is a violation of a home, which is a sacred space. It leaves feelings of extreme vulnerability. That homeowner is likely buying alarm systems, adding locks to the doors, sleeping with the lights on, or even not sleeping at all, anxious over every creak or bump in the night. A thief with empathy would direct the apology toward those feelings: "I'm sorry I violated your home, your safety and security. I am sorry I disturbed your peace."

Finding empathy is hard. After all, if you really considered other people's feelings, if you really felt what they felt, you would have avoided the problem you go into in the first place. Financial swindlers act because of greed to increase their own profit. If they acted as a fellow shareholder or investor, they would never dream of cutting corners or stealing. They would understand their role as stewards of other people's treasures. They would understand that they weren't stealing other people's money but, rather, they were robbing people of their futures.

Empathy requires an emotional transformation. We need not just a change of our minds but often a change of our hearts. When we gain empathy, we can be more visibly in a better position to have our apology received and accepted.

Probably the most famous empathetic transformation in literature comes from Charles Dickens's famous *A Christmas Carol*. Here Ebenezer Scrooge begins as the antagonist, flaunting his miserly attitude, terrorizing his faithful employee Bob Cratchit, and generally serving as the personification of Anti-Christmas. After a night marked by the visit of four ghosts, Scrooge is famously scared straight.

Much is made of how Scrooge's final fright—the witness of his own grave—turned the tide, but the real transformation came from the Ghost of Christmas Present, who took Scrooge to the Christmas Eve home of the Cratchits. Watching the family enjoying their meager Christmas Eve dinner and enjoying themselves, Scrooge saw Cratchit for the first time not as an employee always asking for another piece of coal for warmth but rather as a father, a husband, and a man who had dimensions to his life Scrooge never bothered to notice before. What's more, Scrooge was able to see in flesh what had previously only been the concept of Cratchit's disabled young son, Tiny Tim. It was the witness of Tim that prompted Scrooge's first change. He seemed to understand Cratchit's plight and struggle, marveling that despite the strains on the family—much of it his own doing—the Cratchits seemed to approach their lives with joy. Scrooge's empathy came out of feelings he developed for Tim, true concern. When Scrooge asked what the future held for Tim, he received one of the most famous (and oft misquoted) replies in literature:

> "I see a vacant seat," replied the Ghost, "in the poor chimney-corner, and a crutch without an owner, carefully preserved. If these shadows remain unaltered by the Future, the child will die."

This feeling of empathy set the stage for Scrooge's ultimate transformation. And make no mistake: It was a complete transformation.

> And it was always said of him, that he knew how to keep Christmas well, if any man alive possessed the knowledge. May that be truly said of us, and all of us! And so, as Tiny Tim observed, God bless Us, Every One!

Yes, that's fiction, and we live in the real world, but science suggests that we can find empathy in fiction, particularly if we are having trouble conjuring it through fact. Writing in the *Review of General Psychology* in 1999, Keith Oatley of the University of Toronto noted that our minds can sometimes better explore our own personal feelings when we're putting ourselves in the perspective of characters in books.

"In the simulations of fiction," Oatley wrote, "personal truths can be explored that allow readers to experience emotions—their own emotions—and understand aspects of them that are obscure, in relation to contexts in which the emotions arise." In short, characters in fiction can give us a road map to better understand and contextualize our own feelings.

In fact, fiction gives us the best way to explore a range of different emotions. Within the safety of fiction, we can see feelings, actions, and consequences in a way that allows our own minds to gain a better understanding of our own actions. "Throughout a narrative, it is possible for a reader to move in and out of different perspectives, those of different characters or different perspectives on the overall narrative," Oatley wrote. "There is room in the experience of narrative engagement for the reader to undergo a great deal of psychological movement. Empathy does not interfere with this movement. Its requirement of self-other differentiation ensures that the relationship between readers and characters is not one of complete identity, even in imagination."

Literature isn't the only bit of art to engender emotional transformation. I have trouble holding true sadness myself, so it's been difficult for me to feel empathy for those saddened by my own failings. A few years ago, after a nasty personal breakup, I wanted, for the first time, to "sit" with my sadness. I took it as an opportunity to not try to jump to my own instinct to fix a problem but to be present with my own feelings so I could better approach the reparation I needed to make with some empathy.

Trouble was, I had no idea how to do it. Fortunately, one day while listening to music on a train to Manhattan for work, I heard Gustav Mahler's *Symphony No. 5*, which took up most of my ride that day. Most importantly, and like millions of others around the world, I was enchanted by the Fourth Movement, known commonly as the *Adagietto*. It is widely considered one of the saddest pieces of music ever written. Over the course of several days, in my office and in my home, I played the *Adagietto* over and over. Each time, it was as if pieces of my own feelings were breaking off inside me, becoming separate, clear, visible. At times, I would cry. In the end, though, it allowed me to get the presence of feeling that I wasn't previously emotionally mature enough to even recognize. As I made my own apology at the time, the music would play in the background of my mind. It was a companion, and I believe it put me in a better position to understand the sadness I had caused and work toward avoiding that in the future.

Later, I would find out something fascinating about the piece. (I'm not a classical music aficionado by any stretch. Much of my favorite music came from the 1980s rather than the 1880s.) The *Adagietto* is generally played at times of immense mourning. Famously, Leonard Bernstein conducted the piece in a performance at St. Patrick's Cathedral in New York for the funeral of President John F. Kennedy. But the *Adagietto* was meant to be a love song. As *The New York Times* wrote in 1992:

> The Adagietto served as a love letter from the composer to Alma Schindler, probably shortly before they were married in 1902. The Dutch conductor Willem Mengelberg, in his personal copy of the Fifth Symphony, wrote: "This Adagietto was Gustav Mahler's declaration of love for Alma! Instead of a letter, he sent her this in manuscript form; no other words accompanied it. She understood and wrote to him: He should come!!! (both of them told me this!)." Mengelberg's own description of the Adagietto was "love, a love comes into his life."

And doesn't that make sense? Feelings of sadness and hurt often spring from love. So many of our apologies stem from affairs of the heart. Our emotional responses are often complex and layered. That alone may make it difficult for you to speak with true empathy when you are trying to go beyond sorry. But it is certainly well worth the effort and exploration.

Chapter 4

Delivering the Message

Know Your Audience

One of the most famous apologies in American history is also one that shows the widest range of ways you might have to deliver your message. In the middle of World War II, George S. Patton Jr. was without question America's most notable general in the field, adored as a conquering hero at home for turning around American prospects in Africa and Europe and feared for his cunning and boldness by the Germans. Certainly, he was a colorful man. He was older than most of his peers, entering the army as a horse cavalryman and taking part in what is considered the first "mechanized" military action in US Army history: the punitive expedition led by Gen. John Pershing in 1916 to hunt down Pancho Villa in Mexico. Along the way, Patton competed in the Olympics, built his own sailboat, and sailed it solo from California to Hawaii and even designed an array of uniforms (which the army universally rejected).

Patton was also a man of contrasts. He was patrician and fabulously wealthy, among the richest officers in the army at the time. Yet he connected well with the soldier on the ground, whom he routinely cajoled, pushed, and praised. While much of our modern view of the man came from the 1970 Academy Award winning film, *Patton*, where George C. Scott captured much of Patton's wartime years, the movie didn't quite live up to reality. Interestingly, Patton neither looked nor sounded like Scott's portrayal. He had a rather high-pitched voice, nothing like the gruff and gravelly Scott. That made his speeches quite interesting to hear. While he was known to inspire, he spoke more like a wealthy politician than a foot solider—with one exception: He swore like a longshoreman. "A gentleman should be able to swear for three minutes straight and not repeat himself," he was known to say.

Patton was riding high in August 1943, leading a brutal but ultimately successful Allied campaign to take Sicily, when he visited a group of field hospitals to speak with the wounded. According to Carlo D'Este's biography *Patton: A Genius for War*, Patton was often moved to see the sacrifices made by his wounded men firsthand. He would routinely personally hand out Purple Hearts and pray by the bedsides of the soldiers he met. In two separate visits, on August 3 and August 10, he encountered soldiers who had no visible wounds, privates Charles Kuhl and Paul Bennett. While the circumstances are slightly different, in both cases, Patton confronted the soldiers, asked them what was wrong, and each mentioned their nerves from the shelling. Patton was furious, calling them *yellow bastards*. To Bennett, according to D'Este, he said, "You're a disgrace to the Army and you're going back to the front to fight, although that's too good for you. You ought to be lined up against a wall and shot. In fact, I ought to shoot you myself right now, God damn you." In each case, he then took what would be a defining moment of his career: He slapped them.

It was an offense that would otherwise warrant a court-martial and could have ended Patton's career. (Some critics say it should have.) Interestingly, Patton's value as a general almost made sure the story initially was kept secret. Though hospital staff tried to file a formal complaint, no one forwarded it up the chain of command. General Eisenhower, when he was confronted by journalists about it, arranged for a gentleman's agreement where they wouldn't report it for fear of hurting the war effort. While in the film version, Patton is ordered by Eisenhower to apologize not only to the soldiers but to each of the divisions in Patton's Seventh Army, Eisenhower never went that far. In a private reprimand, he ordered Patton only to "make in the form of apology or otherwise such personal amends to the individuals concerned as may be within your power."

It was Patton who decided to take his apology further. First and foremost, he summoned both Kuhl and Bennett to his headquarters and personally apologized. According to accounts, both were dazzled and pleased by the personal touch, particularly the offer of a handshake. One eyewitness to the Kuhl meeting said his face "lit up with a broad grin. He grabbed and shook the general's hand… It was very impressive and dramatic. I kept thinking, 'My Lord, here is a three-star general apologizing to a lowly private soldier.' I could not imagine anything similar happening in any other army."

Patton then delivered an apology to different groups with varying results. An apology to the hospital staff went over poorly. As one doctor recounted, it was "no apology at all." Different combat units reacted with what D'Este called *quiet indifference.* Yet Patton also likely found strength in the support he got when he addressed some units. Attempting to apologize to the Third Division, soldiers began to shout, "No! General, no, no, no, General, no, no." Patton was moved to tears, ended the speech, and moved on.

Lastly and crucially, one of the most-little-studied apologies from the incident was made to Eisenhower himself. The issue was personal for both of them. Patton and Eisenhower were colleagues and friends. Patton, though senior to Eisenhower through much of his career, respected him as a general and a leader. Eisenhower (as evidenced by his efforts to cover up the slapping incidents) believed Patton was his best general in the field. When he censured Patton, Eisenhower wrote, "No letter that I have been called upon to write in my military career has caused me the mental anguish of this one, not only because of my deep personal friendship for you but because of my admiration for your military qualities."

Patton, while varying in his public apologies between explanation and slight remorse, wrote in his own diaries that he regretted the incident not because of the uproar with the troops but because "I hate to make Ike mad where it is my earnest study to please him."

So it shouldn't be surprising that Patton's best words of apology were reserved for the person he felt he had let down the most: Ike himself. "I am at a loss to find words with which to express my chagrin and grief at having given you, a man to whom I owe everything and for whom I would gladly lay down my life, cause to be displeased with me." Private. Personal. And as history would show, accepted.

We can argue about Patton's words and his sincerity during his apology tour, but one thing was clear: He knew his audiences, and he knew he had to tailor his apologies differently. Face-to-face was vital to the two soldiers he assaulted. They had to see him physically, in a different light, to be in a position to accept or reject the apology. Through the handshake, the hand once used in violence against them turned into a physical form of apology and moving on. Given the vast difference in rank, akin to a god and mortal man, such a gesture mattered. It likely mattered even more than words.

To the various units, Patton likely knew they indeed were indifferent. The outrage from the slap came from two quarters, the hospital staff and the media. There isn't extant evidence the soldiers in the field cared that much. They were more likely to believe Patton's explanation—that he hit the soldiers to set them straight and "fix" their fears—than any apology. In fact, he never talked about a slap in his apologies, instead mentioning "various incidents that should best be forgotten." That was good enough for the troops.

To Eisenhower, to whom he wrote often, a direct letter was the right way to deliver his message. Ike would have expected nothing less. There was a war going on, after all.

How you deliver your apology to go beyond sorry is as important as what you actually say. People you've wronged will look at how you deliver it, whether in person or, if necessary, through video, and decide whether you are indeed sincere. Key to that delivery is an understanding of your audience. In some cases, where appropriate, a private, face-to-face meeting, where you can speak directly to the person you've harmed, is the best way to not only let them hear your words but see your sincerity and experience your empathy. After all, that is facing and owning up to the true harm you caused as you move to beyond sorry. If you're facing widespread public, media, or social media criticism, apologizing in a more public way might be the right way to go. As Patton knew, public apologies are hard to deliver and even harder to get a feel for. In most cases, you never actually see the reaction to them, but they are a necessary component to moving on.

There's often more than one apology you need to make. Most of our transgressions involve different people we've hurt in different ways. One need only look again at Madoff's fraud to see the different kinds of damage he caused. We think about his own investors, the people who believed they had saved and invested for their retirement, only to find out they had nothing. Their lives and futures were shattered by his lies and greed.

But others were hurt too. Madoff's employees lost their jobs, and working at the largest Ponzi scheme in history isn't necessary something on your LinkedIn profile that makes it easier to get another job. Worst of all, Madoff destroyed his own family and its family name. Of his two sons, one died of cancer and the other committed suicide. Madoff's wife quickly changed her name and tried to drift into anonymity. If Madoff were ever inclined to apologize truly, he would have a lot of audiences to reach.

The point is that apologies can never be made in a vacuum. Simply expressing how sorry you are doesn't matter if that sentiment isn't directed at the people you've hurt. Again, if you want to go beyond sorry and be able to heal relationships and get your career, family, or life back on track, you must make an effort to address specifically the people who felt the pain the most. That requires you to deliver your message in the most direct and straightforward way, preferably in person and certainly in a way where people can see you. This gives you the opportunity to not only show your own sincerity but also to again face the personal damage your actions have caused.

The First Seven Seconds

Former FOX News chairman Roger Ailes, for all his controversy and criticism, knew about how humans communicate and respond to communication better than anyone on the planet. To be sure, apologies were not his thing. I worked for him for six years, and the idea of him ever making an apology never came up. When he was facing allegations of sexual harassment, he consistently denied wrongdoing. The company he built, FOX News, apologized on his behalf, but Ailes himself, as far as we know, was defiant until his death.

The irony of that is that Ailes would have known how to deliver a fantastic apology. He knew the showmanship and stagecraft of delivering great messages. He knew that great orations in history were often more performed than uttered. He knew that all words were attached to some context. An avid of collector of historical documents and letters, he would explain, as you walked through his house in Garrison, New York, overlooking the United States Military Academy at West Point, not only what the letters he had framed on his wall said but how they were received in the time they were written. That context and perspective helped him in guiding politicians to victory in launching several television networks and helping business leaders best deliver their messages. Even his most strident detractors and some of those he harmed would admit quickly that he was among the most persuasive and insightful communicators they ever met.

Ailes used to say that people make up their minds about you in the first seven seconds they meet you. Often, this has nothing to do with what you say. They *experience* you, even if you aren't speaking, and those first seven seconds will set the tone for your entire interaction with someone. In his book *You Are the Message: How to Get What You Want by Being Who You Are*, Ailes stressed that when we communicate, we do so with our eyes, our faces, our body language, and our visible attitudes.

"Consciously or unconsciously, we're signaling to other people what our true feelings are and what we really want to happen in an encounter," Ailes wrote. "It's almost a reflex action, like the pupil of an eye reacting to light. People in the presence of others affect each other's bodies. Sometimes imperceptibly, sometimes noticeably, we influence each other's breathing, heart rate, skin temperature, sweat glands, blood pressure, eye blinks, body motions—even the way some tiny hairs stand up on the skin. In the first seven seconds, we also trigger in each other a chain of emotional reactions, ranging from reassurance to fear."

Our very presence as we deliver an apology triggers an emotional reaction in the person we hurt. The best way to deliver an apology is always face-to-face, and the second best is through video. You need to be seen to be believed, after all. But remember that there is a reflexive response to being viewed by the person you've harmed most. In those first few moments, all their negative feelings often come out. People you hurt feel angry, hurt, violated, confused, sad. Your presence before them instantly unleashes all those feelings again. It will be uncomfortable for you to face someone like this, but it is way more uncomfortable for them. You are the one coming into the meeting with a game plan: You want to deliver an apology and work toward a resolution. The people you've harmed have very little idea what to expect or what they want to do. They are in a far more vulnerable position when you deliver your apology. You need to honor that, but it also gives you the opportunity to ensure you're setting the stone.

(Here is one very important caveat: There are certain instances where a personal meeting to deliver the apology isn't appropriate. For instance, if violence was involved there may be legal restrictions that preclude a meeting. Also, the depth of violation the victim feels toward you may run the risk of being compounded by an in-person meeting. Always ask whether you can have a meeting or perhaps a video call. It is their decision to make, but being seen goes a long way toward proving you are sincere in owning your behavior and committing to repair.)

People will see through insincerity, so you cannot simply jump to delivering an in-person apology until you've done the work of going beyond sorry. Your body will betray you if you aren't genuine. How so? Let's take a look at everyday expressions, namely a smile. There are actually two kinds of smiles. One is known as a "social" smile or, worse, the "fake" smile. Those are the ones we usually use when someone is taking a photo, like a headshot or selfie. The other, or the "true" smile, is known as a Duchenne smile by scientists, named after the nineteenth-century French doctor Guillaume Duchenne, who identified it.

There is a physiological difference between the two. A true smile comes when our brain responds to our voluntarily raising the corners of our mouth (known as zygomatic major) while also involuntarily pushing up our cheeks and squinting our eyes. The social smile doesn't have that second reaction, meaning we are smiling with our mouth, but not with our face. That rising of the cheeks, known as orbicularis oculi, is entirely involuntary. We can't fake it.

Interestingly, different parts of our brain control the different types of smiles we have. Researcher Adoree Durayappah-Harrison noted in an article in *Psychology Today* in 2010 that the social, fake smile is controlled by the motor cortex while emotion-related movements, like the Duchenne smile, is controlled by the limbic system, which is the emotional center of the brain.

It's not just a smile—and there will likely be precious few of those during your apology anyway—that can give us away. So many of our own emotions and true feelings are triggered in our face. The first scientific work in this area was done by no less a scientific luminary than Charles Darwin. In 1872, as support for his emerging theory of evolution, Darwin published *The Expression of the Emotions in Man and Animals*, where he argued that emotions and emotional responses were largely universal among different cultures and species as a result of evolution. We're wired to express our emotions facially in very predictable ways. We smile when we are happy. We frown when we're sad. People read our emotional expressions right away because they have the same wiring. Darwin posited this to show the universality of humans, regardless of race and culture. One of the early criticisms of his work on evolution was the Eurocentric belief that Africans and Asians, if they evolved, had different—and inferior—evolutionary paths. But Darwin's work on expressions proved that our evolutionary tendencies ran across the spectrum of race or geography. It also ran across the spectrum of species. When I'm angry, I tend to stick out my lower jaw and snarl. Dogs, wolves, and a range of other animals make similar faces. Animals make similar sad faces as we do.

While major expressions are easy to recognize, we also give ourselves away in what are known as micro expressions, those quick reactions that we often try to control to hide our true feelings. The science of micro expressions has wide use in areas like law enforcement, where investigators are trained to find our involuntary responses to questions before we get ourselves under emotional control and answer, often with less than the truth. Dr. Paul Ekman, an anthropologist, is probably the best-known researcher in this area, building on Darwin's work to identify the universality of emotional expressions. Micro expressions really give a glimpse into your sincerity. They last no more than half a second, but they are noticeable, particularly to someone looking for them. Make no mistake, since the people you've wronged need to believe you to be able to let you move beyond sorry, they will be looking for micro expressions. And these micro expressions will tell more about you than you think.

From the time of Darwin, researchers have focused on a handful of core emotions. The 2015 Pixar film *Inside Out* portrayed some of these beautifully. Joy, Sadness, Anger, Fear, and Disgust played their parts as the young protagonist Riley matured and struggled with the confusing reordering of her emotions as she grew and her life situation changed. Missing from *Inside Out* are two other "core" emotions: contempt and surprise. In his research, Ekman added even more, including contentment, amusement, excitement, embarrassment, relief, guilt, pride, shame, satisfaction, and sensory pleasure.

When we show a micro expression, it is our brain allowing our true emotions to override the emotions we intellectually want to show. No matter how we try to control how people see our true feelings, our brains don't work that way. As Shakespeare's Launcelot said in *The Merchant of Venice*, "at the length the truth will out." Conflict in different parts of our brains open up a crack. We can often get our feelings back under control, but they do show. As someone offering an apology, you'll be especially vulnerable to this. Typically, when we're compelled to apologize, we feel shame at our actions, sadness for the harm we caused, anger at ourselves, worry that our apology will be rejected, embarrassment that we have to seek forgiveness… the list goes on.

Before delivering your apology, ensure that you're in tune with your true feelings because it isn't just a fake smile that gives us away. It's our entire face.

Let's look at our eyes. There is a wide range of research on eye contact, and some of it is contradictory. People who lie tend to try to actually make more eye contact than less, which might suggest you shouldn't look someone in the eye when you're delivering your apology. But people tend to trust someone more when they are looked in the eye, and they are also more likely to feel an emotional connection when they make eye contact. Author Paulo Coelho described the power of eye contact so beautifully in his novel *The Alchemist*:

> And when two such people encounter each other, and their eyes meet, the past and the future become unimportant. There is only that moment, and the incredible certainty that everything under the sun has been written by one hand only. It is the hand that evokes love, and creates a twin soul for every person in the world. Without such love, one's dreams would have no meaning.

The time isn't right to rekindle love when you're delivering an apology. In most cases, that ship has sailed. But the connection that you can make with someone through eye contact is vital to establish what you need most when you say sorry: trust. In 2006, researchers Helene Kreysa, Luise Kessler, and Stefan R. Schweinberger conducted an experiment where participants saw and heard a series of statements that were, by their nature, hard to immediately know whether they were true or false. For instance, one statement was that sniffer dogs couldn't tell the difference between the scents of identical twins. These statements were delivered in two ways: with the person making eye contact and with the person averting their gaze. It turns out that participants were more likely to believe statements by a speaker looking at them directly, compared with someone refusing to look at them. Interestingly, when people were even inclined to disbelieve a statement, they thought twice about it when someone was saying it while looking them in the eye. This suggests, the researchers noted, "the process of rejecting a statement as untrue may be inhibited when that statement is accompanied by direct gaze." The inverse was true as well: Participants were much quicker to reject a statement delivered with an averted gaze.

Even if you're delivering an apology by video, either recorded or live, there's a benefit to eye contact. You should always treat the lens of a camera, phone, or laptop as a real eye. True, you cannot see who is looking back at you, but you will give the perception that you are looking them in the eye. In fact, in Zoom, Facetime, or other video programs, we sometimes have the instinct to look at the video feed of the person we're speaking with. But oddly, while you are looking at them on your screen, they actually don't see that. They see a gaze directed not at your camera—and therefore not at them—but rather directed elsewhere. By looking at their screen, you are averting your eyes from them—a real technological conundrum. I can't stress enough that concentrating on the lens will have an impact.

Researchers have found that simply giving this perception of eye contact will make the interaction more meaningful. A 2006 study on how people respond to sales presentations created identical pitches for a brand of soap. In one pitch, the salesperson looked directly into the camera lens for 30 percent of the presentation, giving the impression they were making eye contact. In another pitch, the salesperson looked away the whole time. When asked to recount details of the presentation, participants recalled a lot more from the one where they were "looked in the eye" than when they weren't. That research has been used since to encourage teachers in remote environments to look at the camera more, so students retain more. Given the emotional depth of the hurt your aggrieved party feels, they're unlikely to forget much about the apology, but the research nonetheless suggests a more meaningful experience when you achieve eye contact.

Of course, eye contact isn't easy. In a face-to-face apology, you are staring into the face of the person whom you have damaged. You can see the anger and the tears. They may hold your gaze, and in their eyes you may see the rage, despair, and sorrow in a way that you didn't expect. You'll likely feel deeper shame, which, in turn, may make it harder for you to look them in the eye. Many people, myself among them, have a habit of smiling when I'm in an uncomfortable conversation. When we are ashamed, it's harder to make or keep eye contact. We're gazing at the rubble our actions left behind, but that very quickly becomes a reflection on ourselves. But you must try to power through those feelings to deliver the apology. Remember, in the soap experiment above, the successful salesperson made eye contact just 30 percent of the time. That was better than nothing. On the other hand, the people you've wronged may not allow you to make or hold eye contact. You might think that lets you off the hook a bit, but it really doesn't. You will have to work harder to create that personal connection; you need to go beyond sorry.

The Public Apology

The harm we cause used to be more localized, but in a world of social media–driven connectedness, our bad actions can play out in front of much larger audiences. In some cases, our transgressions, which may only have affected a few people, can be amplified so that more people are made aware, thus breaking the bond of trust with a wider group. A lot of this reflects the ubiquity of media and the change in what—and whom—we view as important. Time was, only a small number of people merited media attention. Now in the age of influencers, so many individuals are their own media brands. They create content, opine on news, and put their lives on display (for better and, more often, worse) in ways that strangers can consume. What's more, people share what's on their minds more, and that leads to more instances where someone can tweet or post something that offends, more often than not affecting people they don't even know. For the most part, that shouldn't matter. After all, why should we ever care what someone we don't know thinks? Yet anonymous hordes of social media have a way of trying highlight posts they don't like and using them to try to influence their own communities to take action. That's what so-called "cancel culture" is about: Find someone who somehow offends you, and then go after that person's company or business partners and try to ensure that they pay. It's created a crisis minefield, and it's disgustingly formulaic. People will post a quote retweet, tagging an employer, demanding someone be fired for a remark or, worse, a political point of view.

In situations where you feel like an apology will help, the way you say sorry is now more akin to the public apology that celebrities and politicians have been making for years. Public apologies are by their very nature impersonal. It's very hard to be personal when you're addressing an audience of people you don't even know. But it can be done.

The trick is making the impersonal somehow personal. One of the best examples was in 2014, when New York Yankees third baseman Alex Rodriguez was suspended by Major League Baseball for an entire season after he was named among players who used performance-enhancing drugs and human growth hormone acquired from a company called Biogenesis. This lapse was an obvious letdown for the team's owners, other players, and especially the fans. The incident required an apology to everyone affected.

Before spring training for the 2015 season, A-Rod decided to write a note. It wasn't an email sent by a publicist or a tweet. It was an actual, real-life note, written in bold blue ink by his own hand on clean white paper and directed at the fans. The letter was genius in its form, giving the impression that everyone could have gotten such a letter, whether he knew you or not. It also helped that it was written so well:

To the Fans,

I take full responsibility for the mistakes that led to my suspension for the 2014 season. I regret that my actions made the situation worse than it needed to be. To Major League Baseball, the Yankees, the Steinbrenner family, the Players Association, and you, the fans, I can only say I'm sorry.

I accept the fact that many of you will not believe my apology or anything that I say at this point. I understand why, and that's on me. It was gracious of the Yankees to offer me the use of Yankee Stadium for this apology, but I decided that next time I am in Yankee Stadium, I should be in pinstripes doing my job.

I served the longest suspension in the history of the league for PED use. The Commissioner has said the matter is over. The Players Association has said the same. The Yankees have said the next step is to play baseball.

I'm ready to put this chapter behind me and play some ball.

This game has been my single biggest passion since I was a teenager. When I go to spring training, I will do everything I can to be the best player and teammate possible, earn a spot on the Yankees and help us win.

Sincerely,
Alex

The personal nature of that note helped—mostly because it came across as being personal. Any attempt to cut corners here can backfire. The Notes app found on smartphones allows you to create the illusion that you're writing something down, but no one believes that you did. Infamously, singer Justin Timberlake tried his own apology note through Notes and failed miserably. In 2020, the documentary *Framing Britney Spears* premiered, which painted Timberlake in a very unfavorable light for the way he treated Spears, whom he dated but split with in 2002. (He referred to her once as "just some bitch.") The film raised some social media criticism for how Timberlake also never owned up to hurting Janet Jackson's career when, during the 20054 Super Bowl halftime show, he ripped off part of Jackson's clothing, exposing her breast on live television.

Both events were worthy of apology even years later. On the surface, Timberlake's words were fine: "I am deeply sorry for the times in my life where my actions contributed to the problem, where I spoke out of turn or did not speak up for what was right," Timberlake wrote. "I understand that I fell short in these moments and in many others and benefited from a system that condones misogyny and racism." While it was a public apology to his fans, he also specifically mentioned Spears and Jackson "because I care for and respect these women and I know I failed."

It would have been an appropriate *mea culpa*, except he decided to do it using Notes and posting it on Instagram, which made it look cheesy and insincere. The pushback was brutal. Social media lit up with criticism that focused on the way he posted the public apology rather than the substance of it. *Saturday Night Live* lampooned it viciously—poking fun at apologies in general. In a skit, actress Chloe Fineman portrayed Spears herself as the host of a talk show designed where famous people do nothing but apologize. Seconds into the sketch, the faux Spears says, "I'd like to give a quick shout-out to our sponsor, the Notes app. Are you looking to post a lame apology twenty years late? Go through the motions with the Notes app."

As you know from earlier in this chapter, the ability for someone to see you apologize often makes the difference, so don't be afraid to make a public apology more personal by doing it on camera. Give people the opportunity to see your eyes, your expressions, and your emotions. Posting a video that shows your sincerity can go a long way toward having people believe you. Remember to think of the lens on your computer or smartphone as a human eye, and keep contact with that. There's an added benefit: You can maintain control over the message. Shoot multiple takes and discard anything where you feel you've missed the mark. Seek advice from close friends or advisers because they are usually better equipped at judging an apology than you are. Get honest feedback and apply it. Only release an apology video when you are sure it is the best you can do.

Interestingly, the ubiquity of video nowadays is quickly creating a danger point. So many celebrity influencers, when caught in crisis, respond with a quick homemade video that's often characterized less by sincerity than by tone deafness, narcissism, and an eagerness to change the subject. Worse, many influencers use video apologies on sites like YouTube not to make amends but to actually sell products or build followers. As *Vice* put it so well in a 2019 article, "The apology video and its many spin-offs are intentional, purposeful, and increasingly unavoidable—maybe that's why they feel so scripted and hard to believe. In the bigger context of a scandal, it all feels a little like a season of a bad reality show: a narrative arc where conflict builds into redemption until everyone, somehow, is friends again, with viewers meant to keep following problematic stars because, well, they apologized. We have the major villains and the minor, and everyone is vying for a few seconds of screen time."

You, as someone who wants to go beyond sorry, should aim higher. After all, your end game is to be able to move on and earn forgiveness. As we will explore next, that's the hard part.

Chapter 5

The Ideal of Forgiveness

Why It's So Hard

There wasn't much joy in the short life of Maria Goretti. Born in 1890 into extreme poverty, her father, when she was just six years old, tried to eke out a better life for his wife and children by moving from the west side of Italy to the east, hoping that the farmland and work opportunities there were more favorable. Three years after the move, he contracted malaria and died. That forced her mother out into the fields to be the breadwinner and left Maria, then nine, to take on most of the responsibilities at home for her siblings.

It also left her alone far too often with a much older neighbor, Alessandro Serenelli. He would often make crude and sexual comments, attempt to touch her, and do other things, but she resisted. When Maria was just shy of her twelfth birthday, Serenelli, himself twenty, forced himself on her, trying to rape her. She resisted, and an enraged Serenelli turned from sexual deviant into cold-blooded murderer, stabbing her several times.

As she lay in the hospital dying, her last words, reportedly, were, "I forgive Alessandro Serenelli…and I want him with me in heaven forever."

The gesture of forgiveness turned a headline-grabbing tragedy into a story of hope. Sentenced to prison and initially unrepentant, Serenelli later claimed the ghost of little Maria visited him and spoke with him. When he was ultimately released, nearly thirty years after the crime, he seemed to be a changed man. On Christmas in 1934, he went to ask forgiveness of Maria's mother, Assunta, who told him, "If Maria forgives you and God forgives you, how can I not also forgive you?" She also made the gesture of treating him as if he were her own son.

Maria became one of the youngest saints in the Catholic Church. It's believed that her canonization was the only time in history a martyr's mother and killer both took part in the ceremony. She is the patron saint of purity. She is prayed to by rape victims, girls, and teenage girls, and naturally, she is the Catholic Church's patron saint of forgiveness.

Maria Goretti is a saint. Most of us ain't. The example of forgiveness laid out by St. Maria, where she told her own killer she forgave her and then wanted to make sure her God forgave him too, is truly extraordinary and obviously worthy of sainthood. We are not so worthy. The fact that you're reading this means you probably need a better path to make up for some transgressions in your life. But it also means that you want to make good. You care. You are beyond sorry. But you need to know that there was only one Maria Goretti, and her example was rare enough to merit sainthood. People are not naturally wired to forgive. We hold people responsible for their actions for a long time. We remember.

In many ways, it can be cultural. Growing up, my own family talked about "Irish Alzheimer's," where you forget everything but the grudges. Irish Christmas was viewed as an opportunity to gather and silently resent the people we love most. (Perhaps that's why Sigmund Freud said the Irish were the only people impervious to psychoanalysis.) In that environment, there's not a lot of room to forgive. In fact, it rarely comes to mind. Why bother worrying about what forgiveness looks like and feels like when it's an ideal we can never reach anyone?

It's important to remember that forgiveness isn't always attainable. For all the work you put into your apology and your own path for redemption and reacceptance into whatever communities you alienated, people may never forgive you for what you did. You have to accept that. True forgiveness is an ideal to be strived for, but there is never a guarantee you will ever get it. And that's okay. Like all ideals, forgiveness exists as a goal, a star on the horizon to sail your ship by. In the musical *Man of La Mancha*, Miguel de Cervantes, portraying Don Quixote to his cellmates, sings,

> This is my quest,
> to follow that star,
> no matter how hopeless,
> no matter how far.

And later, he sings:

> And I know, if I only be true,
> To this glorious quest,
> That my heart, will lie peaceful and calm,
> When I'm laid to my rest.

The song is actually known as *The Quest*, but it's known by its more common other name, *The Impossible Dream*. Quixote, whose own name now is synonymous with following crazy, improbable dreams, knew that it wasn't important to ever reach his goal, but the glory for him was in the attempt. Indeed, in Cervantes's book, Quixote, while ridiculed for madness, ultimately shows that it's the world around him that is equally mad for not following what seems impossible or even improbable. "When life itself seems lunatic, who knows where madness lies?" Cervantes wrote. "Perhaps to be too practical is madness. To surrender dreams—this may be madness. Too much sanity may be madness—and maddest of all: to see life as it is, and not as it should be."

When you set out to apologize, reform, and renew your life, your quest will surely seem like an impossible dream. But you have no choice. There is no redemption, no reconciliation without at least trying to find forgiveness from the people you've hurt. You may never change their minds, but that's no reason not to attempt the apology and the work that needs to happen.

After all, it isn't about whether you get the credit from others for your work. Going beyond sorry isn't some prize to win but rather a process to reconcile with those you have alienated. You are not looking for credit for the work you have done but rather, quite simply, the joy of even partial redemption.

Why People Don't Forgive

"But I said I'm sorry!"

Anyone with children knows the magic kids think happens when they say sorry. We often demand an apology from our kids, mostly to teach them a lesson so they don't ever do whatever it was that got them in trouble again. (Invariably, they do.) Being sorry is what we ask for, but what kids often expect is instant forgiveness, an instant clean slate where we forget, and though they probably don't fully understand the concept, we forgive.

Forgiving kids is easy. They are, after all, our flesh and blood, and we generally see our own mistakes in them. But when you're forced to apologize in a business or personal context, forgiveness is rare. It's just human nature. Many people to whom we issue an apology are in no position to forgive. They're often too sore over what happened, or they are still feeling the emotional pain of our actions to really forgive us. True, they may say they forgive you, but the truth is they can't. Not so easily at least.

Believe it or not, there is tremendous pressure on people to forgive—and not just from the people seeking forgiveness. It happens frequently in business. When, say, a successful head of sales is accused of misconduct, businesses often seek forgiveness to make the problem go away so they can move past the incident and restore the earning power that executive once provided. In the early 1990s, the United Way—one of America's most-recognizable and powerful charities—was rocked by disclosures that its longtime CEO, William Aramony, used company funds to spend lavishly on mistresses, buy properties in Miami and New York, and take gambling trips to Las Vegas. Worst of all, one of Aramony's mistresses turned out to be a seventeen-year-old girl who had just graduated from high school before their assignations began. Aramony, fifty-nine at the time, bought her a fax machine with United Way money so she could send love letters to his office. As the allegations mounted, it became clear that Aramony's importance in the organization allowed his behavior to flourish, and people were pressured to accept personal, private apologies for the good of all the people United Way supported.

Sometimes the pressure to accept forgiveness comes from our own communities. When incidents like an affair happen personally, friends and family who are rooting for reconciliation often push for it, mostly to take the drama and stress out of their own lives. Because folks around us feel uncomfortable, they want the problem to go away and figure that as long as one spouse apologizes, the other should simply accept it, and that will make the whole issue better.

Religion, likely for good intention, exacerbates the pressure to forgive. Some faith traditions tell us that if we don't forgive others, we can never (ever, ever) expect to get forgiveness from others. Christian scripture is very clear on a responsibility to forgive. Jesus himself, in the Book of Matthew, is quoted as saying, "For if you forgive other people when they sin against you, your Heavenly Father will also forgive you. But if you do not forgive others their sins, your Father will not forgive your sins."

In Chassidic Judaism, there is a belief that *nekemah*, which is the seeking of revenge against another, and *netirah*, the holding of grudges, are both so corrosive to you that they are prohibited under Jewish law. As a result, good Jews, rabbis have taught, should work to ignore the wrong committed against them, act like it never happened, and change their point of view to no longer feel wronged. Why? Because holding onto anger is akin, in Chassidic Judaism, to worshipping false idols—the idol in this case being the religious belief that you can control what is already ordained by God. So it is a *mitzvah*—a Commandment—to forgive.

That's some big-time, straight-from-heaven pressure to forgive. But it isn't necessarily realistic. With my apologies to the divine, we are human, after all. When we're harmed, we have very human reactions. We are hurt. We are angry. We are confused. We feel loss. We mourn the loss of trust we once had. Those don't go away easily. No matter how good the apology is, we don't automatically get forgiveness.

And that's the way it should be. If we are honest with ourselves, we know forgiveness is something to be earned. We can never expect it. We have to understand that we may never achieve it. Forgiveness is the ideal that we should seek, but we can never demand or expect. To do so would be to rob the people we have wronged of their natural emotions and the right to process our transgressions in a way that works best for their hearts and their minds. That simply compounds the wrong rather than promotes the right.

"Though society pressures you to forgive the person who wronged you, the truth is that forgiving may be the worst thing you can do," wrote Deborah Schurman-Kauflin in *Psychology Today*. "Many religions and therapies focus on forgiving a perpetrator so that the victim can 'move on.' The goal is to make sure that the victim does not become fixated on the hurt. This element is critical because if you become completely obsessed with your victimization, you will not be able to function. That is a fact. Fixating freezes you."

Forgiveness, after all, is a process. And the transgressed should never be forced to forgive even if your apology is sincere. This is especially true with severe trauma. A rape victim should never be forced to forgive—or even expected to ever forgive—given all that has been stolen from her already. There is so much to process, so much healing still needed within her, that dealing with your forgiveness should be very low on her list of priorities. Saying sorry may help you, but it would hurt her, given where she is in her own process.

"Don't give in to peer pressure," Schurman-Kauflin wrote. "Don't say you forgive someone when you don't. It won't make you feel better, and it won't make your life easier. On the contrary, it is not about making your life easier when someone asks you to forgive. The purpose behind the question of forgiving is to make the person asking the question feel better."

That isn't to say that people should never forgive, either. There sometimes is as much pain held for failing to forgive as there is from forgiving too soon. But that isn't up to you to dictate. You've done enough wrong already.

We mentioned that in Judaism, to forgive is a *mitzvah*, which is a commandment. But the word *mitzvah* is also synonymous with a good deed, and that's an important framework for your mind as you seek forgiveness and reconciliation. Forgiveness is a gift to you, a good deed from another party who has no responsibility to offer you anything. The etymology of forgiveness makes it clear that it is a gift. *Forgive* comes from the Saxon words that mean just that: to give you something. The English synonym, *pardon*, comes from the Latin *per-donare*, which means to give something away completely. And that's really what we are asking for: We are asking people to give us a gift. That gift may be a second chance. That gift might be a new job. That gift may be overlooking something small we have done where we let someone down. More often than not, that gift is a fresh way of thinking and an avoidance of any biases our actions might have created in others. You will never receive a greater gift because in truth, it is so hard for the giver to make that offer.

So you might be asking whether all of this just makes your transgressions worse. If indeed forgiveness is a gift, it is also an ideal that is damn near next to impossible to achieve. Are we setting ourselves up for a Sisyphean nightmare where forgiveness is always right before us, but we can never enjoy it? Well, no. Part of your responsibility as someone who wants to move beyond sorry is to seek the gift and then accept what you get.

When I was a kid, like all little ones, I tore into the presents under our Christmas tree the minute I stumbled out of bed. It was an orgy of wrapping paper and pine needles when it was all done, and for the most part, I got the toys I wanted or enough of what I didn't think to ask for to make me happy. Invariably, though, we would go to family's houses around the holidays, and there was always an aunt or two who thought it was a good idea to give me a pair of pants or a sweater. Ingrate that I was at the tender age of eight, I would lift them out of the box and say something like "Ugh. Clothes!" My mother was horrified and rightfully embarrassed. So after I had done this frequently enough to strain the limits of her temper, she told me that we had a new rule for presents. Whether I liked it or not, I was always to say, "Just what I always wanted!" I'm sure the look on my face gave away how I really felt, but the words I used were always right for the script. (I've even found myself doing that into adulthood.)

No matter what level of forgiveness is offered, you should treat it as if it is exactly what you wanted. That forgiveness is even on the table, that you are even in a position to ask for someone's pardon, is a gift. Enjoy it. Don't force it. You cannot control the feelings of others, but you can certainly live a life worthy of the gift of forgiveness if you put in the work and stay on the journey.

Forgiving Yourself

You also need to forgive yourself. It fascinates me how often our religious and cultural underpinnings conflict sometimes with psychology. The concept of self-forgiveness is one of those. Growing up Catholic, forgiveness of self wasn't something we ever thought about. When you messed up, you were supposed to apologize and make good to the people you wronged. Then you were expected to go to Church, tell the priest in confession, and get absolution on behalf of the Almighty, courtesy of the wave of a blessing and, depending on the severity of the crime, a handful of Hail Marys. Forgiveness was a function of someone else.

If you've been in a reputational crisis or you wrote something boneheaded on Twitter or if you wronged someone personally, the goal obviously is to seek the gift of forgiveness to be able to move on. After all, you are the subject of judgment, and how you navigate that in your professional and personal life will often make a difference in how you proceed. But you should also seek the gift of forgiveness from yourself. While it won't change your situation, it will certainly change your own outlook and let you seek inner strength to move on. "I have learned that the person I have to ask for forgiveness from the most is: myself," said writer and essayist C. JoyBell C. "You must love yourself. You have to forgive yourself, every day, whenever you remember a shortcoming, a flaw, you have to tell yourself 'That's just fine.' You have to forgive yourself so much until you don't even see those things anymore. Because that's what love is like."

When you do wrong, we know that your actions caused alienation with some important community in your life. If you said something inappropriate at work, you may have lost your job. If you were unfaithful to a spouse, you would have been thrown out of your house or family. If you drove drunk, you have lost your ability to drive. If you committed a felony, you have lost your freedom. In all these cases, we've broken the bonds of trust and acceptance with the people around us. We are outcasts, relying only on ourselves.

But we are also alienated *from* ourselves. Unless we have a serious psychological problem, chances are our transgression led immediately to feelings of remorse, guilt and regret. While we sometimes blame others, we know that the art of a great apology needs us to own our actions and facing the consequences. The introspection necessary to be able to find the right words and right feelings around an apology—and to go beyond sorry to move forward—can very easily lead us down the path of self-hate. When we look at the carnage our words or actions create, we know the blood is on our hands, and that can make us recoil from our own selves. We are monsters. We are stupid. We are not worthy of the communities we harmed.

We cannot expect to receive forgiveness if we don't believe that we deserve forgiveness. We will never be worthy of the forgiveness of others if we haven't figured out how to deal with the shame our own actions have caused. This is true whether the shame comes from your actions and even the shame felt by those who have suffered abuse. "The more shame you heal, the more you will be able to see yourself more clearly—the good and the bad," said Beverly Engel, author of *It Wasn't Your Fault: Healing the Shame of Childhood Sexual Abuse Through Self-Compassion.* "You will be able to recognize and admit how you have harmed yourself and others. Your relationships with others will change and deepen. More importantly, your relationship with yourself will improve."

While engaging in therapy is often a good start, a little self-directed self-reflection never hurt anyone, and increasingly, business leaders are learning that simply to be good executives and managers of people, self-forgiveness can be used to lower barriers to high performance. CEO and small-business coach Rhett Power believes that the exploration of what we need to forgive in ourselves can help release emotional baggage that impedes our success. Writing in *Inc.*, Power suggested five questions to guide this introspection:

1. Can anything be done to change what happened?
2. Do I allow myself to make mistakes?
3. Have I done everything possible to make things right?
4. Why am I holding on to this?
5. How can I use this as an opportunity to grow?

For the purposes of moving beyond sorry, questions no. 3 and no. 5 are probably the most helpful. If you are in a position where you need to make a profound apology, you know you can't change the situation and it isn't necessarily relevant whether you allow yourself to make mistakes. You've made them. But a focus on all the work you're doing to make the situation right is a path to self-forgiveness. If the outcome of your work is some kind of personal or professional redemption, focusing on ensuring that you have done everything in your power to make amends and atone is important. The knowledge of your own actions to repair and heal can form the basis on how you can forgive yourself. After all, those will be the core metrics on which others will base their forgiveness of you.

Likewise, when we ask ourselves how we can find opportunities to grow from this, we're laying out the path for how we move on. As we'll explore in the next chapter, the key to really earning back people's trust comes from how we hold ourselves accountable to the action steps we've made to ensure we're back on the straight and narrow and how we live our lives transparently and openly to show people we are worthy of their love and respect. People may never forget what we've done to wrong them, but they will certainly have the confidence we won't make the same mistakes twice if we show we have learned and grown as a result. If we spend time thinking about those opportunities for growth, we can more easily forgive ourselves for your failures.

I want to spend a moment on Power's no. 4, asking why we hold onto things. This will vary from person to person and from situation to situation. But I find it a useful question because it tells us a lot about what motivates us in the first place. Success is a big driver for people, particularly within executive leadership. They want to succeed, they want professional mobility, and they want financial growth for themselves and their partners. When a reputational crisis occurs, the trajectory of their success is interrupted. That's often the cause of tremendous self-loathing. The world was our oyster, and we got in our own way. So many of us feel a sense of loss of what could have been in our careers. It's a function of how our bad action changes our plans and destroys our trajectory. When we think in these terms, we become slaves to our own "what ifs," replaying the past in our minds rather than planning for the future.

That's dangerous because it gets in the way of the personal reconciliation we need to earn the forgiveness of others. Understanding your motivations—the "whys" of our life that drive us—is very important because the "whys" are the pathway to moving forward. If you're motivated by providing for your family and you lost a job or failed to get a promotion, you must position your path to forgiveness in a way that allows you to get another—potentially better—job over time. If you're motivated by the admiration of the crowd, as many celebrities are, you must position your path to forgiveness in a way that allows you to rebuild your fan base. If you're a politician who is truly motivated by public service (one assumes such a creature exists), you must position your path to forgiveness in a way that earns the trust of voters. Our motivations hold the answer to why we hold onto our self-hate too long. Take this as an opportunity to understand it so you can focus on your "why" instead of on your "what if."

Lastly, remember that nothing and no one is perfect. In the context of going beyond sorry, you can't expect to reach the ideal of forgiveness through the ideal of perfection. That's a sucker's trap. Yes, there's a danger in using the nobody's-perfect cliché as an excuse for your misdeeds, but you also probably don't do your good deeds perfectly either. You are not perfect. You are flawed. I am certainly flawed. We all are. Our ability to forgive ourselves and move on from the crises we created, the hurt we have caused, and the alienation we engendered have nothing to do with trying to be perfect. Rather, by seeking self-forgiveness to make us stronger and allow us to better understand with empathy the pain we have caused to craft the right apology and find redemption, we're in a much better position to actually attain the pardon of others through the acceptance of the faults in ourselves and in our actions.

As Leonard Cohen so artfully sang,

> Ring the bells that still can ring
> Forget your perfect offering
> There is a crack, a crack in everything
> That's how the light gets in.

Chapter 6

Moving Forward

"There is a way to be good again."

It's one of the most gripping lines in Khaled Hosseini's 2003 novel *The Kite Runner*. The protagonist, Amir, is contacted decades after leaving his native Afghanistan by his father Baba's best friend, Rahim Khan, asking him to return to help the son of his best friend in childhood, Hassan. The thought of Hassan, who was raised almost as a brother to Amir, has haunted Amir through his adulthood. Jealous of the love and attention Hassan received from Baba, Amir had once done nothing as another boy, Assef, viciously beat and raped Hassan. The shame of his own cowardice caused Amir to commit an even worse act: He attempted to frame Hassan for theft—particularly heinous since theft is something Baba believes is the only sin in mankind—and though forgiven, Hassan and his father leave, removing the shame of Amir's inaction but leaving behind the inevitable guilt for his own monstrous acts.

The offer from Rahim marks a chance for redemption for Amir, who has struggled with trying to escape his past. "(I)t's wrong what they say about the past, I've learned, about how you can bury it," Amir says, "Because the past claws its way out." Indeed, Amir does attempt to save Hassan's son, Sohrab, who has been sold into slavery to the Taliban. Amir is beaten in the attempt to free Sohreb, an attempt that's ultimately successful—and, for Amir, enlightening. "My body was broken—just how badly I wouldn't find out until later—but I felt healed," Amir said, "Healed at last."

Amir found a way to be good again.

Your own path to redemption doesn't necessarily need to suffer a few broken ribs, but it does require a confrontation. That's why you did so much work in examining your conscience and doing what you can do to seek forgiveness, most importantly the forgiveness of yourself. You don't want to live in a state where you're constantly in conflict with yourself and your past bad acts. You want to truly be free of the worst of what you've done. Like Amir framing Hassan, the act of deflecting to simply push your misdeeds away never works. Making amends, seeking atonement, is vital to being able to be at peace somewhat. Just as you seek to heal others from the worst of your actions, you also need to be healed yourself. And as we've discussed, that isn't always easy because you still probably either don't like or don't trust yourself because of the actions you've committed. Even in the process of making amends, you've probably doubted your own ability to actually move forward.

In his memoir *Dry*, writer Augusten Burroughs recounts leaving rehab and deciding to take a first step toward sobriety by pouring away the liquor around him. But he trips over the ceremonial first step on his path to moving on because he can't get out of his own way:

> Freshly brainwashed from rehab, I carry the bottle into the bathroom. I hold it up to the light. See the pretty bottle? Isn't it beautiful? Yes, it's beautiful. I unscrew the cap and pour it into the toilet. I flush twice. And then I think, why did I flush twice? The answer, is of course, because I truly do know myself. I cannot be sure I won't attempt to drink from the toilet, like a dog.

You need to move forward. Notice we aren't talking about "moving on." There's a difference. Moving on denotes that you're putting the past behind you. Moving forward means that you're incorporating all you have learned into getting on a better path, armed with your newfound knowledge and attitude about yourself and your actions to prove to people that you can go beyond the crisis and grow. Moving forward is akin to showing your work in math class. It isn't enough to say you know the answer; you have to demonstrate through your actions that you understand how you got to that answer. Your crisis is never behind you. Rather, it lives with you—not necessarily in a corrosive way but in a way where it spurs constant reminders and tools to prevent you from falling into the same traps that got you in trouble.

The trouble is, your ability to move forward after a crisis requires you to believe you're capable of doing so. There are so many reasons to doubt our ability to move forward. Chances are, your environment is giving you signals that there is no path forward. If your misdeed caused you to lose your job—particularly if your firing was somehow made public—you probably feel like no one will ever hire you or that you can't achieve the same measure of professional success you once had. If your marriage is in tatters because of infidelity, it's natural to think that you will never have the peace and comfort that you enjoyed before the affair. If you have committed a crime, you may feel that your conviction will be the defining moment of your life. Even if you've forgiven yourself and even if you've received the amazing gift of forgiveness from those you've hurt, the past isn't easy. To truly go beyond sorry, you need to move forward. You need to be able to break through the chains of the past and move forward with your life. And the first step of that is believing that you can convert all the hardship and wreckage your actions have caused into true lessons to guide your life and let you live proudly in a new and fresh way.

Of course, we're wired to believe that people can't change. "Leopards don't change their spots" and all that. Indeed, we are conditioned to view people through a lens of what we believe is inherent in their own nature. The famous Aesop fable *The Scorpion and the Frog* is the most common example:

> A scorpion and a frog meet on the bank of
> a stream and the scorpion asks the frog to carry

him across on its back. The frog asks, "How do I know you won't sting me?"

The scorpion says, "Because if I do, I will die, too."

The frog is satisfied, and they set out, but in midstream, the scorpion stings the frog. The frog feels the onset of paralysis and starts to sink, knowing they both will drown, but has just enough time to gasp "Why?"

Replies the scorpion: "It's my nature…"

But people *can* change. For one thing, science teaches us very clearly that our minds are capable of change, provided we put in the work. In fact, our brains are capable of what seems like lasting change. There's a fascinating study centered around cab drivers in London. Driving a taxi isn't an easy job anywhere, but it's next-level difficult in London, where a maze of streets and alleys makes navigation challenging. As a result, taxi drivers in London have taken an incredibly intense test, known as "the Knowledge." A British neuroscientist, Eleanor Maguire of University College London, wanted to see if the process of undertaking the Knowledge led to any changes in the brain.

Maguire already knew from earlier research that taxi drivers in London taxi drivers had a more robust hippocampus—the area of our brains known for long-term memory—than other people. There also appeared to be some correlation between the size of the hippocampus and how long a person was driving a London cab. But that didn't necessarily mean the size was bigger because of their experience learning the Knowledge. After all, people who naturally had a larger memory center might simply be better conditioned to pass the test rather than learning more along the way. So Maguire decided to study seventy-nine people trying to earn their taxi licenses as well as another thirty-one people not going through taxi training but who had similar demographics and characteristics as the others. All the participants underwent an MRI scan to determine at the start that they all had the same size hippocampus. They also all scored roughly equally on a memory test at the start.

In the end, thirty-nine of the participants ultimately earned their taxi licenses. Crucially, their MRIs showed a larger individual hippocampus for the success drivers than for anyone else—meaning that portion of the brain actually grew over time to accommodate the new necessary knowledge. They also performed far better in follow-up memory tests.

Why is this important for going beyond sorry? Because it shows that biologically we're capable of adaptation and change based on new knowledge. In short, if we can adapt to learn the maze of London streets, we can easily adapt to new thinking and knowledge we need to change our thinking, habits, and behavior after a crisis. We can indeed learn from our mistakes. And we can change as a result.

So we know we are capable of change. If we have a tendency to lie, we are capable of learning to tell the truth. If we steal, we are capable of earning what we want. If we cheat, we are capable of fidelity. If we offend others, we are capable of treating people with dignity and respect. Even if our backgrounds led us to feel conditioned to engage in the worst behaviors we can muster, we are capable of learning to move forward in a better way. We have done the work of owning our bad actions, trying to make amends and pledging to be on a different path. Now it's time to move forward and show the rest of the world that we are successful in living life differently.

Moving from Shame to Accountability

Even if we agree that we can change to move forward, a tendency toward shame can often get in the way. It's little wonder. Shame is a natural reaction to our own behavior. We're ashamed we have let our friends, families, and coworkers down. We're ashamed of ourselves. Shame is an awful feeling. It isn't so much a reminder of the pain we caused as it is a cudgel we use to constantly beat up ourselves emotionally. Rather than believe we're capable of change, shame tells us we don't deserve happiness or forgiveness or redemption, so change won't work. Shame makes us sabotage our own happiness. Shame can prevent us from moving forward. Shame is the enemy of going beyond sorry.

You cannot let the shame you feel from your actions get in the way of moving forward and showing the world that you have learned and changed. If we let shame of our actions in the past define the actions of our future, we will never move forward. We will be stuck in our own heads and in our old ways. Shame will either cripple you into inaction or cause us to second-guess every decision we make as we try to move forward.

No one articulates this better than University of Houston professor Brene Brown. Brown's well-known research is grounded in the study of shame, so it isn't surprising that she has put shame in the best context for us to understand. In *Daring Greatly* (and other works), Brown talks about the "Shame 1-2-3s":

1. We all have it. Shame is universal and one of the most primitive human emotions that we experience. The only people who don't experience shame lack the capacity for empathy and human connection.
2. We're all afraid to talk about shame.
3. The less we talk about shame, the more control it has over our lives.

Interestingly, Brown has written that shame comes from a fear of disconnection, and as we've discussed, most crisis situations that lead to the need for an apology create a situation where we are disconnected. To atone, you will recall, means to be "at one" again with our communities. Yet shame directs us to believe we're abandoned by these communities.

Shame also prompts us to abandon ourselves. Because of shame, we're prevented from believing we're worthy of reconnection with our best selves and the communities or people we hurt. That prevents us from truly making amends and atoning. How? Because you cannot move forward credibly if you're doing so in fear or shame, if you actually don't believe that you're capable and worthy of living a better life and not making the same mistakes over and over again. Shame, according to Brown, is "the intensely painful feeling or experience of believing that we are flawed and therefore unworthy of love and belonging."

It is hard work to overcome shame to believe you are worthy of connection and acceptance. If you've been the victim of a cancel culture–type separation from a job or friendships, you might question whether you're worthy. If you're sleeping on a friend's couch because of a relationship failure, you might question your worthiness. It's natural. But here's an important point to remember: The fact that you're willing to go beyond sorry, to do the work, and to make the commitment to move forward is evidence that you deserve acceptance. You chose to not simply say sorry and hope other people move on from what you've done. You chose to go beyond sorry. You want to make amends for your actions, not get a free pass. You don't want to rub a genie's lantern and make everything go away. You want to evolve and grow and truly live a life worthy of a forgiveness you know in your heart you may not ever be granted. You're opening yourself to change and even the potential for rejection because you know it's the right path—the only path, really—to redeeming yourself personally and professionally and healing the relationships you've ruined. That's brave! By your actions and intentions, you are worthy of acceptance and that should be what you remind yourself when, inevitably, shame creeps in. The work of going beyond sorry can be a vaccine against this feeling of shame.

Moving forward requires shifting your tendency toward shame and moving it toward accountability. There is nothing wrong with being held accountable for your actions. If you truly want to go beyond sorry, you welcome systemic accountability. Like a student who has studied for an exam, you don't have anxiety about the test but an excitement that you're going to ace it.

Shame and accountability are like distant cousins, part of the same family but often with very different lives and experiences. Shame is personal. When we want to shame someone (or ourselves), we make it personal: *You* are bad. *You* are a liar. *You* are a thief. You don't know how to be in a relationship. When we want to hold someone accountable, we focus on the actions: You *did something* wrong. Focusing on accountability allows us to get less personal and more focused on the outcomes we want and need. Instead of telling ourselves that we aren't worthy or capable of moving forward, we can actually quantify that journey by setting up systems of accountability to measure our progress. You can't manage what you can't measure, and a system of accountability gives us the ability to see our progress and gives us ammunition to use when shame creeps into our brains.

This will also help you make the noise go away that will surround you even as you move forward. If you had a public misstep, one fueled by social media interest, there will be people, many of whom you don't even know, who will be constantly reminding you of your shortcomings. Social media is a cesspool of anonymous toxic criticism, and that demonic cheering section is targeting your tendency toward shame. A program of accountability will give you something to focus on and allow you to ignore your detractors and focus on your progress.

What does it mean to focus on accountability? It means to focus on *what* you're doing rather than *who* you are. In some cases, you're putting the focus on what *not* to do. If you've been caught in an affair, avoiding situations where you are alone with someone should be part of your program of accountability. Everyone's program of accountability will be different, but it's important to build one based on the actions that led you to your crisis.

Getting started, it's important to take stock of where you are in your journey. By now, since you've truly examined your conscience and committed to going in a better direction, you should start by reminding yourself of what you need to avoid. Here are some helpful questions to ask yourself as you get started:

1. What behaviors or actions precipitated the event for which I had to apologize?
2. How many of those behaviors and actions do I still engage in?
3. Which people within my circle of friends, coworkers or acquaintances contributed to my bad behavior?

4. How susceptible am I to reengaging in the behaviors that got me in trouble in the first place?

Accountability isn't a look back. Nor is it a look forward. Accountability is about living in the present, ensuring that you're managing your day-to-day thoughts, activities, and behaviors. It's very hard to stop ourselves in a moment or measure ourselves in real-time, but you should at least try. Very often, when we say something we shouldn't, we *know* we shouldn't say it. That little voice in our heads tells us we shouldn't say it. But even though we hear that voice, we very often don't listen.

You have to listen. As you hold yourself accountable to show the world that you're worthy of forgiveness, that voice will be your internal guide, the music of your conscience, in the present, in the moment, and if you just listen and pause and let it guide you, it will be easy to show that you have moved forward from your crisis.

By the way, that little voice in your head isn't a sign that you're crazy. In fact, there's a whole body of science around it. That voice is known as "inner speech," which is essentially us having a conversation with ourselves before we ever let the words leave our lips. First identified in the early twentieth century by Russian psychologist Lev Vygotsky, inner speech has been found to be vital for our own development. It's a guide. It allows us to debate problems and gauge experiences before we verbalize our findings. As the great neurologist and author Oliver Sacks (of *Awakenings* fame) wrote in his book *Seeing Voices*, our inner voice is indispensable for our growth and development. "'We are our language,' it is often said; but our real language, our real identity, lies in inner speech, in that ceaseless stream and generation of meaning that constitutes the individual mind," Sachs wrote. "It is through inner speech that the child develops his own concepts and meanings; it is through inner speech that he achieves his own identity; it is through inner speech, finally, that he constructs his own world."

In the moment, in the present, our inner voice is helping us evolve. Our inner voice—provided we are committed to our work— is a great guide to hold us accountable. As a tool to our learning and personal evolution, there's no better way to keep yourself accountable to your journey to move forward than to listen to your inner voice.

Accountability demands process. How we embark on this change matters. In many ways, you should think of moving forward as more of an evolution than a revolution. Indeed, there's a difference between standard change and evolutionary change. Embarking on dramatic change can be counterproductive. As leadership expert Liz Bentley put it:

> To change implies becoming a different person or changing a significant characteristic. For example, this could entail trying to change someone from being introverted to extraverted. An introverted person prefers to work alone and recharges by doing activities independently. They thrive from solitary time. To change them into an extravert by forcing them to work in constant collaboration with people and/or continually be around people without breaks would push them to work against their natural strengths. It would ultimately not work and make the person very unhappy. They might be able to sustain the change for a short period of time but eventually would go back to their natural style.

Real change takes an evolutionary commitment and revolves around making small changes that can build over time. You cannot change overnight. Modest changes, with accountability along the way, are the best way to ensure that your change is lasting. How small of a change? You can actually look at every action you take in life and view it through the lens of how you are making progress in moving forward from your crisis. In his book *Atomic Habits: An Easy & Proven Way to Build Good Habits & Break Bad Ones*, author James Clear puts the issue in simple terms. "Every action you take," he wrote, "is a vote for the type of person you wish to become. No single instance will transform your beliefs, but as the votes build up, so does the evidence of your new identity."

Isn't that a comforting thought? There's no one large action to take, which by its very nature heightens the danger that the best result is beyond reach. Rather, we can engage in a series of easy-to-accomplish small changes in habit that don't tax us in the moment but pay huge dividends down the line for real reform. We can change our habits, which can change our outlook, which can change our behavior and put us firmly, accountably, and measurably on a path where we have gone beyond sorry, and we can show the world that we are worthy of some measure of redemption. We can move forward in tiny steps.

"All big things come from small beginnings," Clear says. "The seed of every habit is a single, tiny decision. But as that decision is repeated, a habit sprouts and grows stronger. Roots entrench themselves and branches grow. The task of breaking a bad habit is like uprooting a powerful oak within us. And the task of building a good habit is like cultivating a delicate flower one day at a time."

Think small about your changes in behavior. Hold yourself accountable to small steps. And you will go far.

Living Worthy of Redemption

Like Caesar's wife, you need to be beyond reproach. That expression comes from a Roman-era political sex scandal. In 51 BC, according to the Roman historian Plutarch, Julius Caesar was confronted with a problem about his second wife, Pompeia. Pompeia threw what should have been the safest of ladies' nights, a fete to celebrate chastity and fertility for fellow women. Trouble was, a man named Publius Clodius Pulcher attended with an eye toward seducing Pompeia. It's not clear whether he was successful. In fact, most of the evidence is that he wasn't. But Caesar divorced her anyway, famously saying that his wife, of all wives, "must be above suspicion." She was, in Caesar's mind, in a position where no one could ever question her fidelity.

People will watch your behavior more closely after you screw up and even after you're suspected of doing wrong. So you have to fly straight. Perhaps the most egregious example of how *not* to behave in a crisis in recent times has been former New York congressman Anthony Weiner. In fact, Weiner's saga is very instructive in how not to behave in a crisis so you can avoid creating an even bigger one.

In the spring of 2011, Weiner was a rising star in Congress and the Democratic Party. Quick-witted and combative, he was a frequent guest on the politically charged cable television wars and was a force to be reckoned with. He brought New York City charm and bluster to the national stage. What's more, he was part of the most recognized Democratic power couple, newly married to Huma Abedin, deputy chief of staff and close confidant to then-Secretary of State Hillary Clinton.

Then a photo of what appeared to be a man's crotch in underwear appeared briefly on Weiner's Twitter account. Though it was quickly taken down, bloggers began reporting on the photo, which was apparently directed at a twenty-one-year-old college student in Bellingham, Washington. As news broke of the photo, Weiner at first painted himself as a victim. As many folks do when they're caught in a social media scandal, Weiner claimed he was hacked in unequivocal terms: "Look, this is a prank and not a terribly creative one." He made jokes about the incident, clearly downplaying it. "I'm not sure I want to put national, federal resources into trying to figure out who posted a picture on Weiner's website, uh, whatever," he told reporters. "I'm not really sure it rises, no pun intended, to that level."

In fact, Weiner seemed almost nonchalant about it, telling the media, "I was hacked. It happens to people. You move on."

The media, however, did not move on. Weiner was repeatedly questioned about the photo, and he then began evading the questions, ultimately suggesting it was a hit job perpetrated by political rivals to ruin him. Weiner claimed to have hired a law firm and security firm to investigate what he insisted was still hacking, and typical of his take-no-prisoners style, he threatened action: "If it turns out there's something larger going on here, we'll take the requisite steps," he told reporters.

And then he gave up the charade and finally owned up. In what was actually a very strongly worded apology, Weiner admitted fault and showed empathy directly to the people he hurt: "To be clear, the picture was of me, and I sent it," he said. "I'm deeply sorry for the pain this has caused my wife and our family, my constituents, my friends, my supporters, and my staff." Interestingly, he owned up to more than what had been reported, admitting in a tearful statement that he had several "inappropriate conversations conducted over Twitter, Facebook, email, and occasionally on the phone" with women online. He vowed to stay in Congress and, like many men caught in infidelity, swore he would recommit and refocus on his wife and family. It was a solid textbook apology, setting him up to move ahead with his career and find redemption, particularly since many had floated his name to replace Mike Bloomberg as mayor of New York City.

Weiner's plans changed just a month after his apology, when he announced he would be "seeking treatment" for his issues amid the release of several more photos Weiner took of himself and may have sent to other women. That prompted his resignation from Congress with another expression of remorse at the damage he caused around him. "I am announcing my resignation from Congress so my colleagues can get back to work, my neighbors can choose a new representative, and most important, so that my wife and I can continue to heal from the damage I have caused," he told reporters.

Weiner was not done. Nearly two years later, he asked for a second chance. He had reason to believe it was already granted. His wife, Huma, had stood by his side during his self-imposed exile from public life. The couple had a child together, and polls showed him with a shot to become mayor. So Weiner, in May 2013, announced he was seeking the job, saying the past was behind him. "Look, I've made some big mistakes, and I know I've let a lot of people down. But I've also learned some tough lessons," Weiner said in his announcement. "I'm running for mayor because I've been fighting for the middle class and those struggling to make it for my entire life. And I hope I get a second chance to work for you."

Any halo for Weiner lasted just two months. New evidence emerged that rather than learn lessons, Weiner continued sending inappropriate content to women online even after his resignation. Voters wrote him off, seeing how he had blown his second chance. He finished fifth in the Democratic primary. And it got even worse. In 2016, the *Daily Mail* disclosed Weiner had sent sexually inappropriate messages to a fifteen-year-old girl. That led to an FBI investigation, which ultimately yielded charges. He pled guilty to and served time in federal prison for charges of sending sexually explicit images and directions to engage in sexual conduct with the girl. His wife, naturally, filed for divorce.

Conceivably, someone like Weiner could still stage a comeback, though evidence suggests he doesn't deserve one. Simply being convicted of a crime and serving prison time doesn't preclude you from earning back people's trust and respect—provided you live beyond reproach.

One of the best examples is Michael Milken. He popularized junk bonds when he was at investment firm Drexel Burnham Lambert in the 1980s. They were such a great product that savings-and-loan institutions bought them in droves. When the junk-bond market collapsed, so did the S&Ls. Prosecutors were looking for a scapegoat, and they found one in Milken, who eventually went to jail on charges of insider trading and securities fraud.

Starting in prison, Milken began repositioning his life. A cancer survivor, he became a loud and active champion of medical research. Milken has raised hundreds of millions of dollars for cancer research. He is the ultimate philanthropist, is well-respected in almost every circle, and is a brilliant and innovative thinker. His Milken Institute is one of the greatest collections of thought leadership in the world.

Interestingly, Milken is also a good example of why you might need a solid public relations team around you, too. When I was a journalist, I wrote about Milken and his history. The mention was overwhelmingly positive, focusing on all his good works. No sooner did the story run, though, than I received an email from members of Milken's PR team. Their complaint? That I mentioned his conviction and jail time *at all*. Milken's personal history, they argued, is all about his philanthropy and thought leadership. Mentioning his conviction was out of place. It was the kind of aggressive reputation management I didn't expect—nor will I ever forget.

Others have worn their criminal convictions on their sleeves. One of the most noteworthy examples of someone who found reputational redemption was Charles Colson. At the outset of his problems, Colson, a close adviser to President Richard Nixon, was far from a sympathetic figure. He openly referred to himself as Nixon's "hatchet man" and once said he would "walk over my own grandmother" to get Nixon reelected—which he did in landslide fashion in 1972.

But Colson, like several others in the Nixon administration, ended up being arrested and eventually pled guilty to a charge that he obstructed justice in trying to influence the trail of Pentagon Papers figure Dr. Daniel Ellsburg.

The guilty plea itself was a seminal moment for Colson, one he described, according to his *Washington Post* obituary, as "a price I had to pay to complete the shedding of my old life and to be free to live the new." The plea came after a religious conversion of sorts, where Colson decided to focus on deeply Christian beliefs. It was the ultimate contrition, a grinding of his entire life prior in order to focus on creating a new one for himself.

After seven months in federal prison, Colson emerged with a new mission: creating a faith-based program for inmates nationwide. In 1976, he started Prison Fellowship, which grew to become the largest prison ministry in the world. The mission of Prison Fellowship was to encourage and support other criminals in getting beyond their pasts and finding hope that there was a future where society could forgive and allow people to truly be rehabilitated. By the time he died in 2012, Colson was widely credited with finding new ways to rehabilitate criminals beyond simply long prison sentences.

Not everyone has to walk a completely different path than they had before. You just have to show that you're committed to not doing wrong again.

As we saw with Anthony Weiner and his inability to stay faithful, most people are willing to give you a second chance and sometimes a third, but you can't push folks' patience. If you are truly willing to go beyond sorry and move forward, you have to show people that you get it and own your actions. You have to live a life beyond not only bad behavior but also beyond suspicion. There invariably will be friends, coworkers, or communities who just will find you hard to trust. As we mentioned when we discussed forgiveness earlier, that's a gift you may never receive. But it will take living a life that is beyond suspicion to get you there.

Living beyond all suspicion seems hard because, well, it is. But there's some good news here, and it speaks directly to the work you have committed to in order to go beyond sorry. Your work should have caused a transformation in you. You should think differently. You should feel differently. You should have a better understanding of yourself and all that motivates you to make decisions and engage in behaviors in your daily life. We know you're capable of change. Living that change is what will set you apart and truly show that you are worthy of redemption and potentially forgiveness. You've done the work to examine what led to your crisis, you have shown true remorse, you've sought atonement with the communities you alienated, and you have offered forgiveness to yourself. After all that, if it is indeed sincere, you have become a different person. That should be visible to the people around you for the rest of your life.

Just like receiving forgiveness, though, it may be hard for others to see or even believe. After all, you've harmed others. Many still feel the pain of your actions. Many are still angry with you. All that is stacked against you to achieve forgiveness when it comes to people believing you've changed, no matter how virtuous you are.

You have to understand that your actions have exacerbated the natural biases people have against you. Don't take it all personally. In fact, we all have biases. But when you wrong someone, you trigger certain cognitive biases that are very hard to overcome. Cognitive biases are the creation of someone else's reality to a situation that differs from the true reality because of their framing of the situation in front of them. These biases are important hurdles of which to be mindful, patient, and understanding as you live your life and move forward.

The most common hurdle will be confirmation bias. That's the tendency of people to look for things that confirm what they already believe rather than see things as they are. Confirmation bias compels people to only seek information that confirms existing beliefs. We've seen this over the past few decades in the media. Based on your political affiliation, you may only watch certain cable news channels simply because they don't challenge your beliefs. You enjoy consuming media that confirms your own point of view and ignores the perspective of others. That tendency is heightened on social media. Chances are, you follow people on Twitter or Facebook who largely share your opinions. You make a choice to indulge your confirmation bias. Even if you follow people with different points of view, you probably discount what they say because of your own point of view.

As someone seeking forgiveness and redemption, it's easy to see how confirmation bias can play out. If you were caught in a lie, the person you harmed will always be looking for you to lie again, not believing anything you say. Even if you tell a half-truth, you will confirm to others that you are a liar. Worse, you will confirm that you will *always* be a liar. That is likely what people believed before, and years of telling the truth consistently won't necessarily change their minds. You can see why living a life beyond reproach is necessary to combat confirmation bias.

There are other cognitive biases at work. The sibling of cognitive bias is hindsight bias. With hindsight bias, we tend to see events that we believe we have somehow predicted. When we say "I knew it all along," we're saying that we predicted behaviors or actions. When we fail on your path to moving forward, people we've harmed in the past will no doubt say that they always knew we would fail. In many ways, their cognitive bias against our personal or professional growth fuels the idea that in retrospect, everyone should have known we were destined for failure.

People have a tendency to believe they're always right, but it's actually more psychologically complex than that. In 2012, researchers Neal Roes of Northwestern University and Kathleen Vohs of the University of Minnesota said there were three levels of this bias. The first level is called memory distortion, which means we actually misremember the circumstances of the past. Then we have inevitability, which is an insistence that some action was just bound to happen. And then finally we go toward foreseeability, which is that we simply knew it all along. So if someone is fired for stealing goods from a company, coworkers will believe that they knew something like that would happen. That creates a hurdle for redemption.

You'll also be subject to what's known as actor-observer bias. This is the tendency of people to see external factors as the blame for their own actions and internal factors as the blame for the actions of others. You may get into a fender bender at a shopping center parking lot and say that the sun got in your eyes, so you were blinded backing up. But you will blame the driver of the other car for not paying attention. You may botch a sales meeting because you believe the slide deck prepared for you wasn't strong enough, or technology somehow failed you and interrupted the flow. But a coworker doing the same presentation would fail in your eyes because she wasn't prepared or didn't do enough research to reach the potential client. In a romantic relationship, one partner may feel that the problems she brought to the relationship were caused by the pressure of raising kids or stress at work. But she will also feel that her partner is somehow not equipped emotionally to deal with their issues or doesn't care or love her enough. People looking to move forward by living a blameless life will always have to overcome the feeling that there is something inside that drives them to bad behavior—even if those judging them engage in the same behavior and justify it on external factors.

You cannot control other people's biases. Everyone lives in their own reality. As you try to make amends, you can't control how people make decisions about you. You're subject to the judgment of others, particularly those whom you've wronged. It's a fact of life and a fact of crisis. And you deserve it. After all, you've owned your actions and know that you deserve to be judged in some way. Yet while you can't control people's biases, you can influence their thinking. By living a life beyond reproach, you will not give them ammunition to fuel those biases.

You're probably better off not worrying about overcoming these biases. That might seem counterproductive since in many ways, you might be trying to redeem a career or save a marriage or friendship. To do that, you have to win over people. But you can't worry about what you can't control. The best you can do is have a clean conscience and be proud of your improved mindset and clean behavior. Your confidence that you've changed and evolved will eventually shine through. Rather than be discouraged by the fight to overcome biases, be energized by your own successes in living a blameless life. Find strength in that. Don't lose sight of the heroic work you're doing to reform your life and make amends. Even if you fail to win back the trust of the people and communities you've wronged, you're in a better position to move on and be additive to new people. You may not save your marriage, but you will show up as a better partner in your next relationship. You may not save your job, but you will be a better leader in a new career or company. All of that is within reach, and all of that can be determined by your own actions and your own growth. You have gone beyond sorry and have become a different, more mindful person. That's the goal. And that's the payoff for doing all the work. Celebrate that. And celebrate you.

Chapter 7

When Not to Apologize

By all accounts, it seemed like nothing more than a simple tweet. In the midst of the COVID-19 outbreak in 2021, people had a range of emotions about and reactions to the disease. There was a ton of information, much of it conflicting. Can wearing a mask protect you? No. Well, yes. In fact, you need one. Cloth will do. Actually, it needs to be surgical. Vaccines? They stop the virus. Well, they might not stop the virus, but your symptoms are milder. Or they may not really protect you from some variants at all. With so much information and confusion, it was little wonder that international debates broke out about how to fight the virus and what policies and behaviors people should engage in.

Predictably, a lot of the information fueled the confirmation bias we discussed in the previous chapter. People were looking to confirm their own feelings about how they should behave during the pandemic. There was a ton of data to parse and analyze. Health experts were honestly torn about what to do, and there were no shortage of opinions and the people debating them. It became a political maelstrom and created a spillover effect on broader social issues. The murder of George Floyd caused civil unrest that tore the United States apart and sparked a conversation about racism and justice. It also caused people to take to the streets, some peacefully and others in violence. Amid this, political conservatives, fueled by images of shops looted and buildings burning, criticized domestic leftist groups like Antifa for taking advantage of the COVID outbreak and anger over social justice to loot and promote anarchy. COVID, politics, and a social reckoning led to strong political polarization of just about everything.

Conservative activist Andy Ngo was one of the most vocal—and controversial—voices against the actions of groups like Antifa during the nationwide George Floyd protests. He wrote a book, *Unmasked: Inside Antifa's Radical Plan to Destroy Democracy*, which was widely praised by the right and panned by the left. Amid the debate over the merits of the book came praise from an unlikely source: Mumford & Sons banjo player Winston Marshall. Marshall tweeted to Ngo, "Finally had the time to read your important book. You're a brave man."

The response to the tweet was swift, with critics saying Marshall was supporting fascism and promoting the far right. He received tens of thousands of tweets and retweets, and several pushed to "cancel" Mumford & Sons for its support of conservative views. It was the kind of controversy only Twitter could simmer and brew.

It was a classic reputational PR crisis for the band, which had otherwise enjoyed a fairly loyal fan base and good-to-neutral sentiment among the public. Marshall's initial response was to issue a statement that seemed tailor-made by a public relations firm trying to quell a social media uproar: "Over the past few days I have come to better understand the pain caused by the book I endorsed. I have offended not only a lot of people I don't know, but also those closest to me, including my bandmates and for that I am truly sorry. As a result of my actions I am taking time away from the band to examine my blind spots. For now, please know that I realize how my endorsements have the potential to be viewed as approvals of hateful, divisive behavior. I apologize, as this was not at all my intention."

But then Marshall thought about it a bit more. He wasn't trying to embrace an ideology. He liked a book. In fact, Marshall was an avid reader and often tweeted to authors about books he liked. Rather than take a side, he was naïve about the impact of the tweet.

"I failed to foresee that my commenting on a book critical of the Far-Left could be interpreted as approval of the equally abhorrent Far-Right," he would later write.

And he wasn't a fascist and was offended to be painted as one. "Thirteen members of my family were murdered in the concentration camps of the Holocaust," he wrote. "My Grandma, unlike her cousins, aunts and uncles, survived. She and I were close. My family knows the evils of fascism painfully well. To say the least. To call me 'fascist' was ludicrous beyond belief."

As he thought about it, he felt he really had nothing to apologize for. He had apologized because his band's name and reputation were being skewered as a result of his tweet, but he didn't, in retrospect, feel his own actions deserved the attacks or warranted the kind of apology he had made.

So he took it back.

In a blog post, he announced he was leaving Mumford & Sons and was no longer sorry. "I have spent much time reflecting, reading and listening," Marshall wrote. "The truth is that my commenting on a book that documents the extreme Far-Left and their activities is in no way an endorsement of the equally repugnant Far-Right. The truth is that reporting on extremism at the great risk of endangering oneself is unquestionably brave. I also feel that my previous apology in a small way participates in the lie that such extremism does not exist, or worse, is a force for good."

Why did he apologize in the first place? "'Rub your eyes and purify your heart—and prize above all else in the world those who love you and who wish you well,' Aleksander Solzhenitsyn once wrote. In the mania of the moment I was desperate to protect my bandmates," Marshall said. "The hornets' nest that I had unwittingly hit had unleashed a black-hearted swarm on them and their families. I didn't want them to suffer for my actions, they were my priority."

To save the band and to preserve his conscience's desire to speak freely, Marshall left Mumford & Sons. "The only way forward for me is to leave the band," he said. "I hope in distancing myself from them I am able to speak my mind without them suffering the consequences. I leave with love in my heart and I wish those three boys nothing but the best."

As we know, to go beyond sorry takes work. It starts with owning our actions fully and unreservedly. We have to be genuine in our desire to make amends, deliver our sorrow forcefully, and commit to living in a way where no one can ever accuse us of bad behavior again. At the beginning, though, to go beyond sorry, you have to be, well, sorry. Marshall wasn't. Rather than own his apology, he disowned it. And that was the right call for him.

If you're not sorry, don't say you are. True, there may be reputational reasons to issue an apology. Companies do it almost on a knee-jerk basis now in a way to ease social outrage and protect corporate or executive reputations. That might quell the crisis and check a box for what's expected by the public, but it never sets up a situation to take that apology to the next level and truly reform behavior. Any short-term benefit of a quick apology, no matter how well-written or well-delivered, will ultimately be viewed as hollow if there is no follow-up. It certainly can never be the basis to go beyond sorry and reclaim your reputation. It's simply not genuine. If you want others to believe your apology, you have to believe it yourself.

It's okay to not be sorry and not apologize. In fact, in some cases, not apologizing can be the most honest thing you do. That was certainly the case of Anna Sorokin, the so-called "fake heiress" who was convicted of grand larceny and theft of service in 2019. Sorokin posed as a German heiress to swindle $200,000 from banks and businesses. It was a story made for the New York tabloids: a woman without scruple or mercy who conned some of the biggest names and banks in Manhattan. Though she was sentenced to four to twelve years in prison after her conviction, she was released early in good behavior and proceeded to profit from her own story. Netflix paid her hundreds of thousands of dollars to dramatize her story, and she documented her post-prison life on Instagram. Like Bernie Madoff, she blamed her victims rather than show remorse. "I just told people what I wanted, and they gave it to me, or I would move on," she told the BBC Newsnight in an interview in 2021.

Rather than feeling remorse, she saw a silver lining to her crime. When asked if crime paid, Sorokin answered simply, "In a way, it did."

In some cases, you can admit you made a mistake but also not go the extra step and apologize, provided you're at peace with the consequences. Jeff Zucker's statement when he abruptly resigned as head of news network CNN is a good example of that. CNN in late 2021 and early 2022 was going through a period of turmoil. The network had fired popular prime-time host Chris Cuomo over the assistance he gave his brother, disgraced former Gov. Andrew Cuomo, during the period when the governor was facing numerous sexual harassment claims. During the investigation into the Cuomo mess, Zucker was asked about whether he was engaged in a sexual relationship with a subordinate, decades-long aide and CNN chief marketing officer, Allison Gollust. Gollust herself had briefly worked for Governor Cuomo in between stints with Zucker. Zucker apparently had not disclosed that relationship, which he was required to do, and was faced with a situation where he could resign or be fired. He chose to step down.

In a memo to the staff announcing his departure, Zucker acknowledged that he had done wrong. "As part of the investigation into Chris Cuomo's tenure at CNN, I was asked about a consensual relationship with my closest colleague, someone I have worked with for more than twenty years," Zucker wrote. "I acknowledged the relationship evolved in recent years. I was required to disclose it when it began, but I didn't. I was wrong."

And he expressed further regret in how the situation played out. "I came to CNN on January 28, 2013," he wrote. "Together, we had nine great years. I certainly wish my tenure here had ended differently. But it was an amazing run. And I loved every minute."

Nowhere in that statement is an apology. Why? It's likely that he wasn't sorry. He has a strong personal relationship with someone he has been close with for two decades. They are romantically involved. That relationship is more important to him than the job. And he likely felt that given his past success, he could either retire comfortably or easily find a new job later. He wasn't contrite. He wasn't defiant. He was at peace with his decisions and the consequences, public as they were. No need to apologize.

Not saying sorry is sometimes harder than actually apologizing. Some people use apologies as a crutch. Many people say they're sorry not only when they aren't remorseful but when they've truly done nothing wrong. We have likely all met people who almost reactively say "I'm sorry" to little things. Ever get an email that starts with "I'm sorry to bother you, but…"? Here, sorry isn't an expression of remorse but rather a defense mechanism to ward off potential rejection. Most people wouldn't be bothered by an email, but in the event you are, you express remorse almost as a shield to a bad reaction.

Some researchers believe excessive apologizing, particularly for no real fault, is an involuntary reaction to anxiety. "Depending on the purpose of the behavior and the context in which it is occurring, it could be conceptualized as a safety behavior, an overprotective behavior, or compensatory strategy," Martin Antony, director of the Anxiety Research and Treatment Lab at Ryerson University, told *Vice* in 2017. "All of these are terms used to describe behaviors that are designed to protect an individual from aversive emotions or potential threat."

Overapologizing for trivial matters also minimizes you. When you tell someone you're sorry, you're essentially taking blame for an action. You're saying sorry because it's your fault. You're admitting you've given some kind of offense to another. Interestingly, there are gender differences here. There's a lot of business leadership and personal-improvement literature around how women generally apologize more than men—and shouldn't. The science is still evolving on the subject, but the clearest work so far came from researchers Karina Schuman and Michael Ross, who in 2010 performed two studies to figure out whether women truly apologized more and why. In the first study, participants were asked to journal how many times they felt they committed offenses and how many times they apologized for those. Men generally reported fewer actual instances of offense than women, but interestingly, the percentage of times each group reported apologizing was roughly the same. So the frequency of apologies was higher for women but only because women felt they had committed more offenses than the men had.

Why is this? Schuman and Ross performed a second study that looked at the offenses themselves. They asked participants to view a series of recalled and imaginary actions and rate them based on how offensive they were. Men were less likely to view these actions as offensive than women were. That meant that men had a higher threshold for what constituted offensive behavior—and thus what warranted an apology. In short, the gender difference was less about an impulse to apologize than about how people viewed what was actually offensive and therefore deserving of an apology.

It's important to understand how this threshold for offensive behavior can make us apologize for things that simply don't warrant it. Why are we taking blame onto ourselves? Rachel Hollis, in her book *Girl, Stop Apologizing: A Shame-Free Plan for Embracing and Achieving Your Goals*, says women in particular are programmed to face life with too much shame. We learn that because we grow up with it all around us. "I don't care what religion you were raised in. You weren't taught guilt and shame by your creator. You were taught guilt and shame by people," Hollis wrote. "That means whatever your people thought was shameful is what you learned to be ashamed of. Whatever your family or the influential people in your life thought was something to feel guilty about is what you have guilt about now."

What's more, Hollis posits, many women view themselves through the lens of others' approval, which lends itself to a bias toward unnecessary apology. "Women are taught that to be a good woman, you need to be good for other people," she wrote. "If your kids are happy, then you're a good mom. If your husband is happy, you're a good wife. How about a good daughter, employee, sister, friend? All of your value is essentially wrapped up in other people's happiness. How can anyone successfully navigate that for a lifetime? How can anyone dream of more? How can anyone follow their what if, if they need someone else to approve of it first?"

The goal, Hollis said, is to "stop apologizing for being who you are and become who you were meant to be."

How does one do this? Well, as the title of her book says, it starts with not saying sorry for every damn thing. How many times have you responded to someone by saying sorry? "Sorry I missed your call." "Sorry to interrupt you." "I'm sorry to tell you this, but…" You're not sorry. You missed a call likely because you were on another one. You are interrupting someone because what you have to say is more important than what they're doing. You are telling someone a hard truth they need to hear, and you're not sorry about it. So stop apologizing when you're not really sorry. All you're doing is taking blame you don't deserve. You're minimizing yourself.

What's more, you're minimizing the power that a true apology can bring you in the future. Overdoing anything takes the exclusivity and meaning out of an action. Do you know someone who is a chronic yeller, screaming over every last thing? It doesn't take long to minimize that yelling in your mind because no matter what you do, you're likely to get yelled at. So why care? When someone gets angry at anything, they're saying they're angry at everything. It becomes a fact of life, something to shrug your shoulders over. The same is true of apologies. When you say sorry all the time, you project that you're sorry about everything. So how do people know when you are truly, madly, deeply sorry?

Saying sorry should be reserved for when you're actually sorry about what you've done. It's basic economics: Items with scarcity have a higher value than items of abundance. When you apologize for everything, it becomes your commodity, something so plentiful that it loses impact when it's delivered. That doesn't mean that you should only apologize for the worst offenses you've committed. Apologies are appropriate in any instance where you've committed an offense against someone or have done wrong. But they shouldn't be uttered as a matter of course or over even small matters. Reserve them so that they maintain their value and power.

Sorry, Not Sorry

There's a great pop-culture middle ground that's emerged where people say, "Sorry, not sorry." It's the opposite of an apology. It's a defiant battle cry, three words that tell someone that they may believe an apology is warranted, but it isn't coming. It is acceptance of an offense, a punctuation that there was no offense for which to take blame but rather the blame was on the person demanding some kind of offering of regret.

Singer Demi Lovato popularized the phrase in their 2017 hit song *Sorry Not Sorry*.

> Baby, I'm sorry (I'm not sorry)
> Baby, I'm sorry (I'm not sorry)
> Bein' so bad got me feelin' so good
> Showin' you up like I knew that I would
> Baby, I'm sorry (I'm not sorry)
> Baby, I'm sorry (I'm not sorry)
> Feelin' inspired 'cause the tables have turned
> Yeah, I'm on fire and I know that it burns

The song is Lovato's anthem of revenge, a balefire against shame. The song's origins come from the very public fight Lovato, a former child actor, had with mental illness and substance abuse. Lovato had their share of critics for nearly every aspect of their life. Lovato got too fat. Lovato's sexuality was wrong. Lovato's voice was overrated. While many people in the public eye invariably suffer public scrutiny (it comes with the territory, after all), Lovato seemed to get it worse than others, and their own reactions to it showed the deep psychological toll it had taken.

So what did Lovato do? Rather than back down to the hate, Lovato did what singers do and sang their lungs out. "You want me to apologize? Too damn bad. Sure, I'll say sorry if it will make you feel better, but you sure as hell better know that I am not sorry. I have a complicated life, one you can't imagine from the comfort of your couch, and I am dealing with it in my own way, with my own work, and with my own love of self. What is there to apologize for?"

Payback is a bad bitch
And baby, I'm the baddest

In addition to the shield to shame, the use of "Sorry, not sorry" injects a measure of humor into an otherwise tense situation. Humor too is a great antidote to shame or conflict. No one turned horror on its head better than actor, director, comedian, and genius Mel Brooks. So many of his works involved Adolf Hitler, a character in history not known as a comic fool. Brooks's famous play *The Producers* featured the fake musical *Springtime for Hitler: A Gay Romp with Adolf and Eva at Berchtesgaden.* Brooks's remake of *To Be or Not to Be* saw Brooks portray an actor portraying Hitler himself. The end of *History of the World, Part I* teases a segment of Hitler on Ice with the dictator figure skating. Hitler was a monster, the embodiment of evil with the blood of more than six million Jews on his hands, including the lives of people close to Brooks himself. There is nothing funny or whimsical about Hitler. He remains the embodiment of an evil not seen since Lucifer himself fell from heaven.

Yet Brooks portrayed him often, and many in the Jewish community had mixed feelings. Some were confused. Some were outraged. Some, predictably, called for him to apologize. When Brooks released *The Producers* in 1967, "Every rabbi in the world sent me a letter," Brooks told NPR in 2018. Rather than apologize, Brooks owned it, so much so that he claimed that he answered every letter with a letter of his own. "I said, 'Listen, get on a soapbox with Hitler, you're gonna lose—he was a great orator. But if you can make fun of him, if you can have people laugh at him, you win,'" Brooks said.

Think of that. Hitler was a monster, but his evil became flaccid once Brooks imbued his legacy with humor. Hitler tried to destroy the Jews, and Brooks, almost single-handedly, disarmed that by making him less a subject of scorn as one of ridicule. That's real power.

Taking the "Sorry, not sorry" approach does that. It also, in a way, helps you fight the impulse to apologize when saying sorry isn't appropriate. When I started this book, I thought about all the different societal pressures that give us feelings of shame and how those cause us to apologize so often. God knows I've had reason to issue real apologies in my life and to enter the process of trying to go beyond sorry. I'm human, after all, with all the flaws and incompleteness that entails. But I've also been one of those people who probably said sorry when I didn't have to or didn't mean it. As I looked at the pressures to apologize around me, I came back to one of my favorite childhood games: Hasbro's SORRY!

Remember that game? The goal is to move four of your pawns around a board and get to a safe space at Home. Along the way, your pawns are supposed to land on those of your opponent and knock them out, sending them back to Start. Interestingly, the game is based on a centuries-old Indian game called Pachisi. (There's an American version that's close, called Parcheesi from Parker Brothers, not Hasbro.) The word *pachisi* comes from the Hindi to represent the number 25, which is the largest number of squares your piece can move. But when the British coopted and commercialized the game in 1929, the name chosen was designed to target the feeling winning players would have: It's called SORRY! because it's assumed that you're sorry for bumping off your opponents. To win, you have to knock off everybody else. But why should someone feel sorry for that? That's the ultimate reason to *not* say sorry. Why apologize for winning? That's the goal of the game. (For that matter, it's the goal of life.)

In many ways, true competitors know that SORRY! is actually "Sorry, Not Sorry." And Hasbro did something clever. It recently released an adult-themed board game called—wait for it!—SORRY! NOT SORRY! It's essentially the original, except you can sabotage your opponents and use NOT SORRY! cards to make them tell you "have you ever"–type secrets about things they did in their lives. The idea is to have fun with the intimacy of our own foibles, indiscretions, and mistakes. We're encouraged in the game to share our petty misdeeds, our one-night stands—anything we generally prefer not to share in polite company. The game is liberating. Rather than shame, we air a measure of vulnerability to our fellow players. Sure, I slept with that loser in college, but I'm not sorry about it! You want me to be sorry? I'm wearing that as a badge. Even if I regretted something, I learned from it, and it made me stronger. Why be sorry about it?

In the end, being "Sorry, not sorry" about a situation is far better in some circumstances than crawling on your knees for forgiveness. If you've truly hurt others, then do the work to go beyond sorry. But if you insist on acceding to the conditioning around you that made you make apologizing a knee-jerk response to quotidian offenses, save your breath. Own it. Laugh at it. And stop living your life by the judgment of others. You're better than that.

The Long Arm of the Law

If you've committed an actual crime or engaged in behavior with a legal ramification, there are special situations that make issuing an apology dangerous. Let's say you drove drunk, crashed into another car, and did serious bodily and property harm to someone else. You know you're at fault. You drank too much and made the reckless and dangerous move to get behind the wheel when you were impaired. If you are a good, decent, moral person, your instinct will be to apologize and offer a true statement of contrition that takes you beyond sorry.

But if you have an attorney worth his or her salt, they will tell you to say nothing. Well-known Florida defense attorney Matthew Shafran notes that it's important to remember the words uttered when a police officer reads you your rights: Anything you say can and will be used against you. If you immediately apologize, the other party could, in theory, take that as an admission of fault. A good lawyer may be able to work around it in a criminal case, but you can take it to the bank that a lawyer suing you for civil damages (where there's a different legal standard for proof) will use that to his or her advantage. In fact, Shafran notes, in the case of any situation like this, it's vital to actually say nothing. In drunken-driving cases, Shafran even goes so far as to suggest not submitting to a sobriety test or saying anything at all since that is only likely to confirm that you were too stewed to get behind the wheel. From a criminal-defense standpoint, lawyers want to get you through the incident and put the actual case behind you before you embark on your journey to go beyond sorry. You can be sorry, but when police or opposing counsel is around, keep it to yourself.

Apologies in the legal realm typically come during sentencing, only after you've been convicted of a crime. Indeed, US federal sentencing guidelines take remorse into consideration. In some cases, sincerely apologizing and acknowledging contrition can actually lead to significant reductions in penalties. In a comprehensive study of the relationship between apologies and the US legal system, Stephanos Bibos of the University of Iowa College of Law and Richard Bierschbach of Yeshiva University noted that "judges reduce sentences by two or three levels for defendants who express contrition or remorse. At the high end of the Federal Sentencing Guidelines, this reduction can subtract years from a defendant's sentence." It happens at the state level too. When the death penalty is in play, a defendant's perceived remorse can significantly reduce the likelihood that a jury will impose the death penalty, the researchers said.

There's also an ongoing debate over whether physicians and medical professionals should apologize when they make an error. This is a complicated issue. Doctors carry with them an ethical obligation to their patients. The American Medical Association's Code of Ethics says physicians must "be honest in all professional interactions" and "regard responsibility to the patient as paramount." Of course, doctors are human, so they make mistakes. There's a reason you never want to hear "oops" in an operating room. Mistakes that a doctor makes can have lasting health consequences—up to and including the death of a patient. Doctors have an obligation to be honest with their patients and own up to their errors. But such an admission could leave them open to an acceptance of responsibility in a medical malpractice case.

That's why many states have adopted what's known as apology laws. These shield doctors from liability from those statements in the event of a lawsuit. They allow a physician to maintain a level of honesty and trust in care and not have that be held against them in court. It also lets hospitals and health care providers be aggressive about tracking and remediating medical errors, with an eye toward avoiding malpractice cases in the first place.

That, however, doesn't mean doctors should be quick to say sorry. Sometimes medical mistakes happen beyond the control of the physician in charge. And depending on the state, courts grade the strength and depth of apologies for whether they even qualify under apology laws. For their part, doctors don't seem eager to jump to apologize. Writing in *The Journal of the American Academy of Psychiatry and the Law*, researchers Nina Ross and William Newman noted that surveys have shown 95 percent of physicians indicated that they felt obligated to tell patients about a medical mistake based on their code of ethics and their responsibilities to their patients. Yet only 41 percent of actually said they had disclosed minor harmful errors to their patients. What's more, just 5 percent disclosed major errors. "Clearly, a discrepancy exists between physicians' desire to disclose and their practice of disclosing errors," the researchers noted.

In truth, the safe approach while litigation is pending is usually to be very careful about apology. There's no doubt it raises the possibility that the legal implications of your bad actions might get worse. Though there has been more research into the role that apologies can have in legal matters, it remains an evolving area of the law. At issue, of course, is whether the legal system is about rehabilitation or retribution. Do we want to lock up offenders and throw away the key, or do we want to believe that our corrections and justice system exists to help people learn, make restitution, and come out better citizens and humans for the experience? Find that answer, and the role of apologies will become much clearer.

Your Comeback

This brings us full circle in going beyond sorry. In an era of so-called cancel culture, in social media mobs, in zero-tolerance environments, is there even a role for rehabilitation after apology? Should an executive who had an affair with a staffer be allowed to hold a position of authority again? Should a politician who took a bribe be able to hold public office again? Should a wife who had an affair be allowed to return to the trust and love of her spouse and children? Should someone's missteps remain searchable on the web for the rest of her life?

These are questions for the sages. But there are enough examples of forgiveness and redemption to give those of us who have failed our communities hope that we can achieve atonement. People want to blame, but they also love a comeback. Deep down, I believe that everyone has made grave mistakes in their lives. I believe everyone has something they have done or said that they hope no one in their community of families and friends ever finds out about. As a result, when these mistakes or errors are exposed in others, they root for some kind of reconciliation and redemption to occur. They want someone else to prove they've warranted a second chance because they themselves may need a second chance and a shot at forgiveness down the line.

Society is conditioned for you to make a comeback even if it might not seem that way on Twitter or in the uncomfortable silence of your own home. That comeback depends on you. You cannot control the outcome, but you can control the work. You can control you. That means acknowledging when an action of yours deserves real contrition and a full apology. That means owning your actions and examining your conscience fully. That means finding the people you've hurt and facing their pain forthrightly. That means living a life beyond suspicion and showing the people around you that you have changed in a way that matches your words. It means moving forward comfortably in your own skin, mind, and heart.

Don't be sorry.

Go beyond sorry.

You've got this.

About the Author

Ray Hennessey is an expert in crisis communications, marketing, and public relations. He is executive partner and chief executive officer of Vocatus, a global marketing and messaging consulting firm. His crisis work focuses on helping executives and individuals overcome reputational challenges while creating a positive narrative that helps build clients' businesses and better their lives.

Previously, he was president and chief executive officer of one of the top fifty largest public relations, marketing, and crisis-response firms in the United States. He is a frequent speaker on the topic of reputation management and digital communications.

With more than twenty-five years of media, marketing, and management experience, Hennessey previously served as editorial director for Entrepreneur Media, helped launch the FOX Business Network, and appeared regularly on CNBC and CBS News. Earlier in his career, he was editor at SmartMoney.com and Dow Jones, where he wrote the IPO Outlook column for the *Wall Street Journal*.

www.ingramcontent.com/pod-product-compliance
Lightning Source LLC
Chambersburg PA
CBHW022019150726
47990CB00002B/721